Social Issues
in Literature

The Food Industry
in Eric Schlosser's
Fast Food Nation

Other Books in the Social Issues in Literature Series:

Social Issues
in Literature

The Food Industry in Eric Schlosser's *Fast Food Nation*

David Haugen and Susan Musser, Book Editors

GALE
CENGAGE Learning·

Detroit • New York • San Francisco • New Haven, Conn • Waterville, Maine • London

Elizabeth Des Chenes, *Director, Publishing Solutions*

© 2013 Greenhaven Press, a part of Gale, Cengage Learning

Gale and Greenhaven Press are registered trademarks used herein under license.

For more information, contact:
Greenhaven Press
27500 Drake Rd.
Farmington Hills, MI 48331-3535
Or you can visit our Internet site at gale.cengage.com

For product information and technology assistance, contact us at

Gale Customer Support, 1-800-877-4253
For permission to use material from this text or product, submit all requests online at
www.cengage.com/permissions

Further permissions questions can be emailed to permissionrequest@cengage.com

Articles in Greenhaven Press anthologies are often edited for length to meet page requirements. In addition, original titles of these works are changed to clearly present the main thesis and to explicitly indicate the author's opinion. Every effort is made to ensure that Greenhaven Press accurately reflects the original intent of the authors. Every effort has been made to trace the owners of copyrighted material.

Cover image © Jeff Morgan 16/Alamy.

LIBRARY OF CONGRESS CATALOGING-IN-PUBLICATION DATA

The food industry in Eric Schlosser's Fast food nation / David Haugen and Susan Musser, book editors.
    p. cm. -- (Social issues in literature)
    Includes bibliographical references and index.
    ISBN 978-0-7377-6381-2 (hardcover) -- ISBN 978-0-7377-6382-9 (pbk.)
    1. Fast food restaurants--United States. 2. Food industry and trade--United States. 3. Convenience foods--United States. 4. Schlosser, Eric Fast food nation. I. Haugen, David M., 1969- II. Musser, Susan. III. Schlosser, Eric Fast food nation.
    TX945.3.F667 2012
    642'.50973--dc23

                                                    2012017725

Printed in Mexico
1 2 3 4 5 6 7 16 15 14 13 12

Contents

Chapter 1: Background on Eric Schlosser

Contemporary Authors

As a veteran journalist, Eric Schlosser's extensive research
on the food industry and working conditions within the
United States has led to the creation of a body of work
shedding light on several largely ignored problems within
the American economy.

Eric Schlosser, as told to Julia Livshin

In an interview, Schlosser tenders his opinions on the
health risks and labor problems inherent in the food industry and the lack of consumer and governmental will
to demand that the system be changed.

Chapter 2: *Fast Food Nation* and the Food Industry

George Ritzer

Fast Food Nation presents an overview of the ways in
which the fast food industry has caused producers and
workers to adopt the same high speed, high efficiency
business practices that fast food restaurants model.

Cecelia Tichi

Many critiques of *Fast Food Nation* mistakenly overlook
the emphasis on worker mistreatment within the food industry. Literature educators should reevaluate this book
and stress the connection it has to other canonical works
that discuss the important social issue of worker-industry
relations.

While making compelling arguments, *Fast Food Nation* ignores the fact that consumers have repeatedly voted with their dollars as to whether the fast food industry should change. In addition, the industry's large size means that it must be particularly responsive to consumer demands.

Chapter 3: Contemporary Perspectives on the Food Industry

A growing awareness of injustices and unsustainability within the food industry has provoked the public and the government to respond to these issues. As a result, farmworkers' wages have increased, small-scale farming has grown, and individual farmers are fighting to halt industrial farm monopolies.

Introduction

Although he had made a name for himself as an investigative reporter for the *Atlantic Monthly* in the 1990s, Eric Schlosser did not rise to widespread public attention until the 2001 publication of his exposé of the food industry titled *Fast Food Nation: The Dark Side of the All-American Meal.* The book remained on the *New York Times* best-seller list for more than two years and also gained comparable rankings in Canada, Great Britain, Japan, and other countries. In a January 21, 2001, review, Rob Walker of the *New York Times Book Review* characterizes *Fast Food Nation* as "an avalanche of facts and observations" about the fast food industry, from meatpacking to the serving of meals. He rightly notes that the book questions not only the health and value of fast food but also the industrialization model that has influenced modern business practices and global culture. In his concluding remarks he writes, "Schlosser makes it hard to go on eating fast food in blissful ignorance." Similar assessments in other journals and newspapers align Schlosser with the famous muckraking writers of the early twentieth century—such as Upton Sinclair, whose novel *The Jungle* (1906) addresses the impoverished lives of immigrant workers and lack of health and safety concerns within the Chicago meatpacking industry. Like Sinclair, Schlosser's early life did not suggest that the talent for journalism was in his blood, but his career, like Sinclair's, is defined by his writings about disadvantaged laborers and the socioeconomic impact of unrestrained capitalism.

Eric Schlosser was born in Manhattan on August 17, 1959. His father, Herbert Schlosser, practiced law for Wall Street firms, but in 1974 he was chosen to serve as president of NBC broadcasting, a position he held until 1978, when he was promoted to executive vice president of NBC's parent company, RCA (Radio Corporation of America). Young Eric and his mother, Judith, were pulled to California to keep pace with Herbert's cross-continental executive duties. When he reached adulthood, Eric entered Princeton University and graduated with a degree in American history. He then went on to do graduate work at Oxford, where he studied British imperial history. Building on his interests in historical subjects and the power of empire, he turned his hand to playwriting in the 1980s and drafted *Americans,* a fictional work that centers on the assassination of President McKinley as an act of resistance to US imperial aims at the turn of the century. The play was not performed, however, until 2003, after Schlosser had gained notoriety for his journalism. After his graduate work in England, he returned to New York in 1992 and secured a job as a script reader and story editor for the actor Robert De Niro's film company Tribeca Productions. Schlosser attempted a few screenplays before publishing his first article in the *Atlantic Monthly.*

His second story for the *Atlantic* focused on the harshness of marijuana laws in the United States. Titled "Reefer Madness," the 1994 piece stirred some controversy and garnered a few negative reactions from readers who believed he was advocating leniency for drug offenders. The experience gave Schlosser the confidence and momentum to leave Tribeca and become a full-time journalist. The following year he penned "In the Strawberry Fields," an award-winning examination of the lives of migrant strawberry pickers toiling for the fruit industry in California. In a June 5, 2009, interview with PBS (Public Broadcasting Service), Schlosser claimed that writing the article "opened my eyes to the difference between what you see in the supermarket and what you see in the fields— the reality of how our food is produced." This *Atlantic* story brought him to the attention of the editors at *Rolling Stone,* who invited him to do a similar exposé on the fast food industry in America. Spending a year gathering research, Schlosser delivered a three-part series of articles that were published in the magazine in 1998 and became seminal chapters in *Fast Food Nation*, the book that catapulted Schlosser to national and international recognition three years later.

Fast Food Nation earned both praise and criticism from reviewers. In a December 2000 appraisal, *Kirkus Reviews* called it "an exemplary blend of polemic and journalism, guaranteed to put you off your lunch." Reviewer Gary Alan Fine countered that he doubted "much of Schlosser's political and economic assessment" of the food industry. Writing for *Reason* in November 2001, Fine noted that most successful and profitable enterprises in America are held up for ridicule, but, he asks, "If everyone hates fast food, how and why does the industry thrive?" Schlosser addresses this issue in a 2002 interview with the *Readers Read* website. "Here in the States, I think, fast food is popular because it's convenient, it's cheap, and it tastes good," Schlosser explains. "But," he continues, "the real cost of eating fast food never appears on the menu. By that I mean the cost of the obesity epidemic fast food has helped to unleash, the social costs of having such a low-wage workforce, and the health costs of the new industrialized agriculture that supplies the big restaurant chains." Schlosser's summary aptly reveals three of the most salient arguments in his book—arguments that have since generated much concern among readers and have even prompted calls for tighter regulation of the industry.

The popularity of *Fast Food Nation* encouraged Schlosser to adapt the work in ways that would reach an even larger audience. In 2006 he wrote the screenplay and produced a feature film version of *Fast Food Nation*. Directed by Richard Linklater, the film resists the obvious documentary format, instead presenting the material in a fictional narrative. Some critics believed the manufactured drama of the film masks and weakens the arguments of the book; others insisted Schlosser's views of the industry still show through the storyline. In the same year, Schlosser teamed up with author

Charles Wilson to publish *Chew on This: Everything You Don't Want to Know About Fast Food*, a repackaging of *Fast Food Nation* for a younger readership. In an interview with the *Book Browse* website, Schlosser maintained that *Chew on This* is intended to make children think critically about their eating habits and to foster hope that alternatives to the fast food industry and its influence exist. "Our aim is to make kids think about what they're eating, where it comes from, and the consequences of every bite," Schlosser told *Book Browse*.

Since the publication of *Fast Food Nation* and its ancillary adaptations, Schlosser has continued to work as a journalist, but he has devoted more time and energy to other tasks as well. In 2003 he published a second book, *Reefer Madness: Sex, Drugs, and Cheap Labor in the American Black Market*, that expanded on the material he had presented nearly a decade before in the *Atlantic*. Living in Southern California, he also kept his hand in the movie business, serving as executive producer of *There Will Be Blood*, the 2007 Academy Award-nominated film by Paul Thomas Anderson. He juggles these interests with his family life, sharing his successes with his wife, Shauna (the daughter of veteran film actor/director Robert Redford), and his two children, Anna and Conor. He has been working for many years on writing a book about incarceration and the prison system. Schlosser refers to it as the third book in his American trilogy (including *Fast Food Nation* and *Reefer Madness*), telling the Inter Press Service in October 2003 that he views the wide scope of these works as "an alternative history of the last 30 years." As *Fast Food Nation* indicates, Schlosser hopes that uncovering this alternative history will encourage people to resist the political and corporate forces that he believes are writing America's future.

Chronology

1959

Eric Schlosser is born to Herbert and Judith Schlosser in Manhattan, New York City, on August 17.

1974

Eric's father, a lawyer and counsel for California National Productions (a subsidiary of NBC), is appointed president of NBC.

1981

Schlosser graduates from Princeton University with a bachelor's degree in American History. He then spends three years at Oxford University in England pursuing studies in British imperialism.

1985

Schlosser marries Shauna Redford, the daughter of actor/director Robert Redford. He writes *Americans*, a play about the McKinley assassination and the beginnings of American imperialism. The play is first performed in 2003 in the United Kingdom.

1991

The Schlossers' first child, Anna, is born.

1992

Schlosser relocates to New York to become a script reader and editor for Tribeca Productions, a film company started by actor Robert De Niro; son Conor is born.

1994

In January, Schlosser's first piece for the *Atlantic Monthly*, "The Bomb Squad: A Visit with the Members of a Police Unit Whose Work Load May Be Growing," is published.

1994–1998

Schlosser writes various articles for the *Atlantic Monthly*, *Rolling Stone*, and *U.S. News & World Report* that will form the basis of his first two books, *Fast Food Nation* and *Reefer Madness*. He wins the 1994 National Magazine Award for Reporting for his *Atlantic Monthly* articles on marijuana laws and the following year receives the Sidney Hillman Foundation Award for his *Atlantic* article "In the Strawberry Fields," an exposé about migrant workers in the California fruit industry.

2001

Houghton Mifflin publishes *Fast Food Nation: The Dark Side of the All-American Meal*, a work that expands on research into the food industry that Schlosser compiled while writing articles for *Rolling Stone*.

2003

Schlosser's second book, *Reefer Madness: Sex, Drugs, and Cheap Labor in the American Black Market*, is published by Mariner Books. The work, which grew out of an *Atlantic Monthly* article, discusses three facets of the United States' underground economy: marijuana, pornography, and cheap labor. He continues to write about these subjects and the fast food industry in the *New York Times*, the *Nation*, and other news journals.

2006

Schlosser and director Richard Linklater bring to the screen a fictional film adaptation of *Fast Food Nation*, starring Greg Kinnear and Wilmer Valderrama. Schlosser wrote the screenplay and produced the film. The same year, Houghton Mifflin publishes *Chew on This: Everything You Don't Want to Know About Fast Food*, a version of *Fast Food Nation* geared to younger readers. The book is coauthored by Schlosser and Charles Wilson.

2007

We the People, Schlosser's play about the Founding Fathers and the drafting of the US Constitution, premieres in the United Kingdom. He also signs on as an executive producer of the Paul Thomas Anderson film *There Will Be Blood*.

2008

Schlosser appears as a commentator in *Food, Inc.*, Robert Kenner's documentary film about agribusiness and corporate farming in the United States.

Background on
Eric Schlosser

Eric Schlosser: Exposing the Underbelly of the US Economy

Contemporary Authors

Contemporary Authors *is an annually updated reference work published by Gale Cengage. It provides biographical details on over 120,000 writers in all genres whose works have been published in the English language.* Contemporary Authors *was originally released as a series of books but is now also available in an online version.*

A reporter for the Atlantic Monthly, *Eric Schlosser garnered public attention in 2001 when he published* Fast Food Nation: The Dark Side of the All-American Meal. *Schlosser's controversial book examined several aspects of the fast food industry in the United States and its global reach, criticizing the large restaurant chains for serving poor quality and unhealthful meals and providing only minimum wage jobs for their numerous employees. Building on the notoriety of this work, Schlosser published a subsequent exposé on fast food's impact on young people,* Chew on This: Everything You Don't Want to Know About Fast Food *(2006), coauthored with Charles Wilson, a writer whose social-issue pieces have been published in major newspapers such as the* New York Times *and the* Washington Post. *Between these two works, Schlosser penned* Reefer Madness: Sex, Drugs, and Cheap Labor in the American Black Market *(2003), an indictment of America's economic underground and the people he claims are abused by its shady activities. In 2006 a film adaptation of* Fast Food Nation *was produced for Fox Searchlight Pictures, bringing Schlosser's message to a larger audience.*

"Eric Schlosser 1960–," *Contemporary Authors*, Gale, vol. 188, 2009, pp. 397–399. © 2009 Cengage Learning. Reproduced by permission.

Investigative reporter Eric Schlosser is a regular correspondent for the *Atlantic Monthly*. Schlosser's first book, the best-selling *Fast Food Nation: The Dark Side of the All-American Meal*, grew out of an article assignment for *Rolling Stone*. The magazine's editors had read one of Schlosser's earlier articles, "In the Strawberry Fields" (which examined the plight of migrant workers and the rise of illegal immigrants in the United States by focusing on the strawberry industry), and were interested in a similar article concentrating on the fast-food business. Schlosser researched the subject extensively, acquiring far more material than was needed for the initial assignment. The result is a book that addresses not only the growing number of fast-food restaurants in America and across the globe, but the numerous effects of the industry on the economy, health, and working conditions in the United States.

Indictment of the Fast Food Industry

As part of his investigation, Schlosser examined the fast-food industry from all angles. His book addresses the quality of the food served, the cleanliness of the restaurants, and the hiring and training of workers, but also looks at the ways in which the fast-food industry is responsible for keeping minimum wages low and how it obtains federal subsidies through franchises. He throws light on the fact that most fast-food employees are teenagers, receiving poor pay and next to no benefits, and that they are twice as likely to be injured on the job than an adult. Then he goes beyond the restaurants themselves and looks at the beef industry, revealing frightening facts about the conditions under which cows are slaughtered at the mind-boggling speed of 400 per hour—approximately four times as quickly as in other cattle-raising nations. Chitrita Banerji, in a review for *American Prospect*, remarked that "the massive amount of information and statistics that Schlosser presents in *Fast Food Nation* might fatigue some readers, but not before making an indelible impression. This book has the potential to turn a couch potato into an activist." *New Statesman* contributor Hugo Miller wrote: "Schlosser knows how to tell a story, and has tapped into a darkly fascinating world that, for most of us, ends at the shiny plastic counters and drink machines." Andrey Slivka, writing for the *American Scholar*, commented: "*Fast Food Nation* is a valuable tool for coming to terms with a corporate consumerism that's become untenable and unsustainable, that acknowledges no moral or natural limits or restraints, that long ago passed a fulcrum point and has grown all-consuming."

Examining America's Underground Economy

With *Reefer Madness: Sex, Drugs, and Cheap Labor in the American Black Market*, Schlosser again returns to material previously addressed in his articles. The book tackles black market commodities of marijuana, pornography, and illegal immigrants in the United States, exploring the growth of an underground economy. Schlosser addresses the ways in which the American public policy of deterrence—preventing crime through the threat of strict punishment and mandatory sentences for specific offenses—actually paves the way for black market operations. Jeffrey Cass, in an article for the *Journal of Popular Culture*, wrote: "With an ethnographer's eye, Schlosser carefully delineates the inconsistencies between the ideological beliefs that govern public policy and the public's insatiable appetite for illegal commodities."

The three sections of the book examine drug laws, particularly regarding marijuana usage; the lives of illegal immigrant workers, specifically those laboring in the strawberry fields of California; and the pornography industry, where the advent of the Internet has caused profits to skyrocket. Michiko Kakutani, in a review for the *New York Times*, found the three arguments disjointed, writing: "While Mr. Schlosser is impas-

Investigative journalist Eric Schlosser at the 2006 Hollywood premiere of the fictionalized film adaptation of his book Fast Food Nation. © David Livingston/Stringer/Getty Images.

sioned and articulate about these inequities, he never pulls his thoughts together into a larger thesis about underground economies and their relationship to mainstream society." But a contributor to *Publishers Weekly* stated: "Like *Fast Food Nation*, this is an eye-opening book, offering the same high level of reporting and research," and Brad Hooper, in a review for *Booklist*, wrote of Schlosser: "His careful research and equally careful writing style contribute to a study that is certain to garner as much attention as his previous book." Dylan Foley, writing for the *Denver Post*, summed up Schlosser's work: "With *Fast Food Nation* and now *Reefer Madness*, Schlosser has established himself as one of the best investigative reporters in America. Whether he is dealing with horribly abused illegal alien workers or people trampled by the drug laws, he [handles] his subjects with wit and compassion."

Addressing a Younger Audience

Speaking with *Grist* Web site writer Sarah van Schagen of the film adaptation of *Fast Food Nation*, Schlosser observed that his work aims to get people to pay attention and to think. "The first step is to just open your eyes and see what's happening," he said, "and I think a lot of my work is driven by that aim." He brings this same purpose to his third book, *Chew on This: Everything You Don't Want to Know about Fast Food*, which repeats *Fast Food Nation*'s argument for a younger readership. As *Chew on This*, written with Charles Wilson, makes clear, fast food has been disastrous for U.S. children and youth—who, as a result of diets filled with soda, chips, and fast-food meals, now suffer from high rates of obesity. But nutritional junk is ubiquitous among American children, the book shows: schools regularly feature soda and candy machines, and fast-food meals are featured on school lunch menus. *Chew on This* covers much of the same material as Schlosser's previous book, but emphasizes the ways in which advertisers exploit the immature minds of young people to turn them into eager and unquestioning consumers of junk food. Examples of the devastation that results from junk diets include the story of a teenage boy who undergoes a stomach-stapling operation to treat his morbid obesity.

Many reviewers felt that the book succeeds in defining the scope and urgency of the problem in terms that young readers would find relevant. But some critics were disappointed that *Chew on This* does not offer more concrete solutions. *Houston Chronicle* contributor Marvin Hoffman, for example, admired the authors' skill in "describing the enormous impact Mc-Donalds and its partners in crime have had on farming and ranching as the demand for millions of tons of potatoes and millions of head of cattle make family operations obsolete," but he added that "there's not too much to latch onto here as sources of change" except a call to boycott fast-food chains—which the critic considered highly unlikely ever to happen. Jeremy Grant, writing in the *Financial Times*, also expressed disappointment that Schlosser and Wilson do not spend more time in the book discussing the efforts of California chef Alice Waters to teach local schoolchildren about growing their own food. Offering a perspective from the food industry, *Restaurants & Institutions* editor-in-chief Patricia B. Dailey criticized Schlosser and Wilson for using "scare tactics" to grab kids' attention, rather than providing readers with a more balanced view of the issue.

A Warning Against Unhealthy Habits

In a *Bakersfield Californian* interview with Emily Hagedorn, Schlosser admitted that the fast-food industry does have some merits. "They prepare meals that are affordable for ordinary people," he pointed out. "They give jobs to a lot of people who no one else would employ. The food tastes good. I'm just trying to encourage them to do all those things . . . but to just do it in a way that isn't so destructive. My aim in writing the book is just to make things better." Explaining to *Advertising*

Age contributor Kate Macarthur that he is not necessarily anti-burger or anti-fries, Schlosser pointed out that "one of every five American toddlers eats French fries every day and that is a public-health disaster in the making. . . . I think children need to be protected from eating unhealthy things for kids." Indeed, he added, he very much enjoys burgers—he just makes sure to buy them at a restaurant whose standards he can respect. "I won't buy anything from the major fast-food chains," he said, "simply because I don't want to give them any money. But my favorite meal is still a cheeseburger, fries and a chocolate shake. In-n-Out is a company with real integrity, and the fries are great. I don't hesitate to eat there."

Unhappy Meals

Eric Schlosser, as told to Julia Livshin

Eric Schlosser is an investigative reporter and author of Fast Food Nation *and other exposés. Julia Livshin, a former staff editor for the* Atlantic Monthly, *was a manuscript reader for the* Atlantic *when she interviewed Schlosser for this piece in 2000.*

In 2000, on the eve of the release of his book Fast Food Nation, *Schlosser was interviewed by Livshin of the* Atlantic. *The following selection is a portion of that interview in which Schlosser discusses the work and the research that went into it. After criticizing the fast food industry for exploiting workers and providing low-nutrition meals to hungry consumers, Schlosser explains his belief that the fast food industry will not change its practices without widespread consumer and governmental action. He insists that because of the dangers posed by handling and cooking raw meat, the government should administer and enforce regulations within meatpacking plants that supply these restaurants and grocery stores and should hold these companies accountable for the products they sell. However, because of the political pull of the food industry, Schlosser worries that tougher laws will not be forthcoming without a larger change in the way the country thinks about food.*

A passage from *Fast Food Nation*, journalist Eric Schlosser's investigation of the fast-food industry, offers the following behind-the-scenes look at the all-American meal:

> The safety of the food seemed to be determined more by the personality of the manager on duty than by the written policies of the chain. Many workers would not eat anything

at their restaurant unless they'd made it themselves. A Taco Bell employee said that food dropped on the floor was often picked up and served. An Arby's employee told me that one kitchen worker never washed his hands at work after doing engine repairs on his car. And several employees at the same McDonald's restaurant in Colorado Springs independently provided details about a cockroach infestation in the milkshake machine and about armies of mice that urinated and defecated on hamburger rolls left out to thaw in the kitchen every night.

Schlosser's book is not just a compendium of kitchen horror stories. In clean, sober prose packed with facts, he strips away the carefully crafted feel-good veneer of fast food and shows how the industry's astounding success has been achieved, and is sustained, at an equally astounding cost—to the nation's health, environment, economy, and culture. . . .

You write that the market for fast food in the United States is becoming increasingly saturated. What sort of future do you see for the fast-food industry? Might it become obsolete?

That's a very good question. In a way, the future of the fast-food industry is tied to the future of this country. If we continue to allow the growth of a low-wage service economy, one in which unions are weak and workers have little say about their working conditions—well, then the fast-food chains will have a bright future. On the other hand, if we bring the minimum wage up to the level it was thirty years ago, in real terms, and we enforce the rules about overtime, and make it easier to organize service workers, the fast-food chains will have to change their business model. Or go out of business. Access to cheap labor, and a lot of it, has been crucial to their success.

I also think that the desire for uniformity and cheapness and reassurance that the American people have had over the last two decades, which has really helped the fast-food chains, could wane. People may become more concerned about what they're eating and reject the idea that everything should be the same everywhere they go. The chains are in a vulnerable position right now, if only because they've expanded so far and wide across the country that they're already reaching the limits of demand for fast food. And if there's a different consciousness in this country, something less conformist, they may really be in trouble.

From an economic standpoint, are the fast-food chains providing something valuable?

Well, there's no question that they're providing jobs for millions of people. At the same time, how good is it ultimately for society to have jobs that are short-term and that essentially provide no training? You could argue that for some teenagers short-term jobs are a good thing as a source of extra income. But I would argue that there should be a major restructuring of the fast-food industry's employment practices so that these aren't just make-work jobs but jobs that actually provide a meaningful kind of training. For the poorest, most disadvantaged people in this society, simply having a job and having some kind of structure in their lives can be useful. But given the tremendous impact that these companies have on our workforce, they can and should provide more than just a place to show up every day.

Another thing that's important to consider is the sort of work that these fast-food jobs have replaced. The old diners and hamburger stands relied on skilled short-order cooks. If you look at the restaurant industry as a whole, jobs at fast-food chains are the lowest paying and have the highest turnover rate. So to the degree that the fast-food companies have grown and thrived and replaced more traditional eating places, they have encouraged the rise of a workforce that is poor, transient, and unskilled.

Same question from the standpoint of food. Fast food is convenient and cheap. Is the fast-food industry providing a valuable service by catering to the consumer needs of a certain segment of society?

There's no question that fast food is inexpensive and easily accessible. For people who don't have time to prepare meals, for households in which both parents work, there's no question it provides a service. But again, at what cost? As I say in the book, the real cost never appears on the menu. The fast-food companies have directed a large amount of their marketing at low-income communities. They are serving extremely high-fat food to people who are at the greatest risk of the health consequences from obesity. They could be selling low cost food that doesn't have the same health consequences, especially for children. The fast-food chains, with their kids' meals and Happy Meals, are creating eating habits that will last a lifetime. And by heavily marketing unhealthy foods to low-income children they are encouraging health problems among the segment of the population that can least afford them.

If you see a change for the better taking place, do you envision these same companies changing their own policies about what they're going to be marketing and holding their suppliers to more stringent food production standards, or do you see a whole new industry taking over?

I think it'll be determined by how easily these companies can change. The McDonald's Corporation, at the moment, in many ways reminds me of the Soviet-era Kremlin. I was unable to get a single question answered after weeks of calling them, e-mailing them, and faxing them. It was what I imagine it must have been like dealing with the old Communist Party bureaucrats. Can the McDonald's Corporation remake itself into a company that behaves ethically, has a stronger social conscience, and changes its menu? That remains to be seen. It may be that new companies will emerge, embodying a different set of values, selling better and healthier food. . . .

You expose some shocking things about the fast-food and meatpacking industries. Did you encounter any resistance when researching this book? Were people hesitant to speak with you?

People were very afraid to speak with me. These meat-packing towns in the High Plains, in Colorado and Nebraska, are really company towns in a way that almost harkens back to the nineteenth century. The meatpacking companies are the biggest employer and most influential employer in town. The workers are often fearful, and rightly so, because so many are illegal immigrants. So it was hard getting access to some of these people and getting them to talk. At the same time, their fear was counterbalanced by their pain, and by their anger at how they're being treated. Once they felt confident about what I was doing and why I was doing it, they were very open with me. Many of them were very brave.

How about the officials at the meatpacking firms and the fast-food chains?

On the whole, they were cordial to me. Some of the fast-food executives and franchisees I met were honorable, good people. Yet at the same time, these are tough companies that do not like to be criticized. So it will be interesting to see if any of them sue me for libel. My book was thoroughly fact-checked and carefully reviewed by a number of attorneys before publication. But the meatpacking industry sure went after Oprah Winfrey a few years ago[1]. And even though she won her case, the Texas law under which she was sued—one of the "veggie libel laws," as they're called—is still on the books. The meatpacking industry has strongly supported these laws, which forbid defamation of agricultural products. Over the past decade, about a dozen states have made it illegal to criticize agricultural commodities in a manner that's inconsistent with "reasonable" scientific evidence. Basically, they give agribusiness companies the ability to threaten critics with expensive lawsuits. In Texas, a man was sued for criticizing the quality of

---

1. Talk show host Oprah Winfrey made disparaging remarks about the beef industry during one of her broadcasts in 1996. Claiming the comments caused a drop in beef sales, the industry took her to court in 1998. Several ranchers from Texas who had launched the suit failed to convince the jury that Oprah was at fault.

a sod company's lawns. In Colorado, breaking the veggie libel law is now a criminal offense. If you say or write the wrong thing about the meat being produced in that state, you could be convicted of a felony. . . .

You warn that "Anyone who brings raw ground beef into his or her kitchen today must regard it as a potential biohazard, one that may carry an extremely dangerous microbe, infectious at an extremely low dose." And you say that the levels of poultry contamination are even higher. How would you respond to someone who has always eaten poultry and ground beef, has never been sick, and who might perceive this as alarmism?

I don't think that I'm being an alarmist. I'm just letting people know what's in their meat. There's no question that the level of contamination in poultry is much, much higher, and the level in ground turkey is highest of all. The pathogens most commonly found in poultry—*Salmonella* and *Campylobacter*—are not as deadly, relatively speaking, as the *E. coli* 0157:H7 that turns up in ground beef. Keep in mind, though, that every year about 30,000 Americans are hospitalized for *Salmonella* and *Campylobacter* infections they got from tainted food. And when the Centers for Disease Control says that there are about 76 million cases of food poisoning in the United States every year, that's not being alarmist. That's a fact.

As for people who think they've never been sickened by ground beef or poultry, my response would be: how do you know? The symptoms of food poisoning often don't appear for days after the contaminated meal was eaten. As a result, most cases of food poisoning are never properly diagnosed. There may be some people with cast-iron stomachs who never get sick, and good for them. But there are millions of people, especially children and the elderly, who are extremely vulnerable to foodborne pathogens.

By the way, I'm not a vegetarian. I have a lot of respect for people who are vegetarian for religious or ethical reasons. De-

Fast Food Nation *author Eric Schlosser (left, facing camera), environmental and international affairs professor Tim Beach (center), and Stonyfield Farm head Gary Hirshberg (right) at the Future of Food conference at Georgetown University on May 4, 2010.* © Tracy A Woodward/The Washington Post/Getty Images.

spite everything I saw and learned while researching this book, I'm still a meat eater. But I don't eat ground beef anymore. I've seen where it comes from and how it's now being made. One of my favorite dishes in the world used to be steak tartare, which is raw ground beef seasoned and then served. I think you'd have to be a great thrill-seeker or out of your mind to eat steak tartare today.

Anywhere?

Just about anywhere. It's unfortunate, but the meat that's being served in fast-food restaurants by the big chains has been more heavily tested than much of the meat that's being sold in supermarkets. And this pathogen, *E. coli* 0157:H7, is very hearty. It lives on kitchen-counter surfaces for days, and the consequences of being infected by it can be truly disastrous. So you have to be very careful when you bring ground beef into your home. That's a sad fact for hamburger lovers, but it's true.

Is it a question of making sure you're cooking it sufficiently?

It's not just a question of how you cook it. It's a question of how you handle it. Anything that the juices of ground beef touch needs to be thoroughly cleaned, and that includes your hands. And again, I've been into these meatpacking plants, I've been into the processing plants, I've spoken to people who have lost children to *E. coli* 0157:H7, and it did not create in me a Howard Hughes–like fear of germs. There are harmful bacteria everywhere and you have to live life fully and you have to eat and you have to shake hands. You could go insane worrying about germs. At the same time, there are certain things that our government could be doing and there are certain precautions that people can be taking that are just common sense. Right now ground beef happens to be a product that may be contaminated with a deadly pathogen, and people should be very careful about how they handle it in their homes. Someone from the CDC told me that the hamburger is a fairly recent invention. And the way that ground beef has been prepared for centuries often involves a long, slow, thorough cooking, as in Bolognese sauce. Cook your ground beef well—or don't eat it. That's my advice.

In the book you quote Upton Sinclair's famous statement about The Jungle's *reception; "I aimed for the public's heart, and by accident I hit it in the stomach." While successful in igniting a public-health scandal, which led to the enactment of food-safety legislation, Sinclair's exposé did nothing to improve the plight of packinghouse workers. If you had to choose, which of the issues in* Fast Food Nation *do you personally feel most strongly about? Where, in your opinion, is the need for regulatory action most urgent?*

Well, ideally, you'd hit both. There is an immediate instinct in most people to worry first about themselves, and that's totally understandable and natural. A large part of the book pertains to food safety and what's in the meat and what we're eating and what the consequences are. It's much more of a challenge to try to get readers to care about other people, about poor and exploited people who are in need of help. I hope the section on meatpacking workers will bring some attention to and empathy for their plight. Of greatest immediate concern to me are the forty to fifty thousand meatpacking workers who are being injured every year and the roughly one hundred thousand Americans, mainly children and the elderly, who are being sickened by dangerous E. coli such as 0157:H7. There are some very simple steps that could be taken very quickly that would reduce the number of injuries in meatpacking and reduce the number of food poisoning cases in the United States. This isn't rocket science. It's technologies and procedures that could be implemented if not tomorrow then next month. The tragedy is they're not being implemented right now because of complacency and greed.

For example?

Well, to improve worker safety, there could be an immediate and tough crackdown on the meatpacking companies by OSHA (the Occupational Safety and Health Administration) and strict enforcement of the worker safety laws that we already have. The easiest step would be to slow down the production line. The big beef slaughterhouses in this country process between 300 and 375, sometimes up to 400 cattle an hour. In Western Europe slaughterhouses tend to slaughter 75 to 100 cattle an hour. In Australia it's about 115. The number of injuries at a plant is often directly related to the speed of the line, so the first thing would be to force these companies to slow down their production lines.

As for food safety, the meatpacking companies should be held strictly accountable for the products that they sell. Manufacturers of stuffed animals are held accountable. The government can force them to recall stuffed animals that are defective and that might choke children. In the same way, the meatpacking companies should be held accountable for the sale of contaminated meat. There should be legislation passed immediately that gives the federal government the power to recall tainted meat. It should not be up to the meatpacking companies to issue voluntary recalls. The federal government should also be given the power to impose large civil fines on meatpacking companies that knowingly ship tainted meat. We should also reorganize the food-safety system in the United States so that there is a single food-safety agency, like there is in many Western European countries. About a dozen federal agencies have jurisdiction over food safety right now. The Department of Agriculture is in charge not only of inspecting our meat, but also of promoting its sale. There's an inherent conflict of interest. We need an independent food-safety agency whose first priority is public health.

In the epilogue you say that the likelihood of such regulatory legislation being passed is slim.

When I wrote the epilogue last spring, the odds were slim. Now they're just about down to none. The meatpacking and restaurant industries work closely with the right-wing Republicans in Congress. Nevertheless, at some point, if enough people demand change and enough pressure is applied, these things could happen. What I'm afraid of is that it might take another large outbreak and a lot of children getting sick for Congress to act.

In the epilogue of the book I also talk about the most immediate way to bring about change, which is through pressure put on the fast-food chains. At the moment the industry is remarkably responsive to consumer demand because the market for fast food is highly saturated and all of the chains are worried about holding on to their customers. The McDonald's Corporation is the world's largest purchaser of beef. I have no doubt that if McDonald's told its suppliers to change their labor practices or their food-safety practices, they would do so—without much delay. Earlier this year, in response to protests by PETA (People for the Ethical Treatment of Animals), McDonald's imposed new rules on its suppliers specifying how livestock should be raised and slaughtered, stressing the humane treatment of animals. The rules set forth how much living space hogs and chickens should be provided, that sort of thing. Well, I'd like McDonald's to take the same sort of interest in the ethical treatment of human beings—in the working conditions and the dangers faced by the people who make their Big Macs.

Looking back at the social impact of journalism at the beginning of the twentieth century, do you believe that investigative journalism today has the same power to effect change?

I'd like to think that it could because that's why I do what I do. At the same time, there are very few places today that are willing to publish serious investigative journalism. *The Atlantic* is not only the best at it, but one of the last. And it's very hard to get readers to care about these subjects. Whatever you write is launched into a political climate, and the political climate for the last twenty years has not been greatly concerned with many of the social issues that concerned people at the turn of the century.

The food safety issue affects everyone. Whatever your political affiliation, you have to eat. But it's much more difficult these days to get readers to care about people who look different from them, speak a different language. I have absolutely no doubt that if the meatpacking workers being crippled and maimed today were blond-haired and blue-eyed, there'd be enormous public outrage. People wouldn't stand for it. This may sound corny, but the time I've spent among migrant farm workers and meatpacking workers has strengthened my belief that all these racial and ethnic distinctions and divisions are absurd. Again and again I've felt a sense of common humanity, of "there but for the grace of God go I." A lot of my writing has tried to give a voice to people outside of the mainstream. I don't expect my sort of journalism to change the world, but if it can add some shred of empathy or understanding or compassion, if it can convey a fraction of what I've seen and learned, it's well worth doing.

Social Issues in Literature

CHAPTER 2

Fast Food Nation and the Food Industry

Fast Food Nation Exposes the Mcdonaldization of the US Food Industry

George Ritzer

George Ritzer is Distinguished University Professor in the Department of Sociology at the University of Maryland and the author of The Mcdonaldization of Society.

In the following viewpoint, Ritzer uses ideas from his own work The Mcdonaldization of Society *(first published in 1993) to discuss Eric Schlosser's* Fast Food Nation. *Ritzer agrees with Schlosser that the fast food industry has created a business model based on speed, volume, and efficiency and has foisted this model upon its suppliers so that the larger food industry has been transformed in how it conducts business. Ritzer claims, however, that Schlosser does not recognize that the fast food industry has also created consumers and employees that, perhaps unconsciously, conform to this model as well, changing their lifestyles and work habits to maximize efficiency and speed. Ritzer also warns readers that such critiques of the industry often fail to account for any positive impacts of the industry model or at least offer a more balanced treatment of these significant social issues.*

*F*ast Food Nation is based on the premise that a nation is what it eats and Americans eat a great deal of fast food. On any given day, about a quarter of adult Americans visit a fast-food restaurant; in 2000, Americans spent $110 billion on fast food (more than on higher education or new cars); 3.5 million people work in the fast-food industry (most being paid the minimum wage). What they eat is generally mediocre

George Ritzer, "Revolutionizing the World of Consumption," *Journal of Consumer Culture*, vol. 2, no. 1, March 2002, pp. 104–111. Copyright © 2002 by SAGE Publications. Reprinted by Permission of SAGE.

(although [Eric] Schlosser likes McDonald's French fries), and is likely to be a health hazard in the short run (e.g. illnesses caused by *e. coli* in the meat) as well as in the long run (high blood pressure, arteriosclerosis, heart disease, stroke related to the high fat and cholesterol levels in much fast food).

Forcing One Model of Food Production

The book's greatest contribution is its discussion of what I would call *vertical McDonaldization*. That is, the enormous success and voracious demands of the fast-food industry have caused other industries throughout its supply chain to McDonaldize in order to meet those demands. That is, the McDonaldization of the fast-food industry, and its massive and continuous demand for supplies, virtually requires that its suppliers achieve something approaching the same level of McDonaldization (thereby closely linking changes in consumption and production) in order to meet that demand. Schlosser goes into great detail about how potato growing, the processing of frozen French fries, poultry raising, cattle ranching and meat packing have all grown far more rationalized. While this has led to dramatic increases in production in all of these industries, that growth has not come without costs. Meat and poultry are more likely to be disease-ridden, small producers and ranchers have been driven out of business, and millions of people have been forced to work in low-paying, demeaning, demanding and sometimes outright dangerous jobs. For example, in the meat-packing industry, safe, unionized, secure, manageable and relatively high-paying jobs in firms with once-household names like Swift and Armour have been replaced by unsafe, non-unionized, insecure, unmanageable and relatively low-paying positions with largely anonymous corporations. While some (largely owners, managers and stockholders) have profited enormously from vertical McDonaldization, far more have been forced into a marginal economic existence.

A Certain Type of Consumer and Employee

While Schlosser implicitly raises the issue of vertical Mc-Donaldization, he does not bring the discussion 'down' to the level of the individual consumer of fast food (and other McDonaldized products). That is, just as the fast-food restaurant pushes McDonaldization 'upward' to the industries that supply it, it is also the case that it presses it 'downward' on those who consume in McDonaldized settings. It seems likely that we are producing McDonaldized consumers in much the same sense that we are producing a McDonaldized meat-packing industry. The effect of eating so many meals in fast-food restaurants is that such consumers become increasingly efficient, predictable, calculable and oriented toward using non-human rather than human technology. More generally, it is likely that such consumers are characterized by just as much irrationality of rationality as the factory farm producing chickens.

Similarly, it could be argued that the fast-food industry is creating McDonaldized workers both within the restaurants and in the various industries that supply what is needed by their vast needs. Employees in the restaurants have to make do with McJobs and those in related industries are forced to work ever more efficiently and predictably; they need to produce more in less time, and they are confronted by an increasing array of non-human technologies which not only control them, but threaten soon to replace them completely. The irrationalities associated with these rational systems have their strongest impact on those who work in them.

Overall, Schlosser has little to say that is good about the fast-food industry (however, many of the problems he discusses were already well known). Nevertheless, tens of millions of Americans flock to fast-food restaurants each day and it is likely that far more than that number do so in other parts of the world. One would like to think that the enormous international popularity of *Fast Food Nation* will help to change that. However, my guess is that Schlosser is largely preaching to the converted and that the tide of consumers of fast food not only in the United States, but throughout the world, is more likely to swell than shrink. Fast food (and its icons) is too well entrenched in people's thoughts and actions and it fits too well with the changing nature of society (for example, the massive entry of females into the labor force), for it to suffer much from the rantings of contemporary muckrakers (in his critique of work in the industries supplying the fast food industry. . . . Schlosser is reminiscent of, among others, Upton Sinclair and [his novel] *The Jungle*). One would like it to be different, but I think it unwise to hold our breaths hoping that Eric Schlosser will replace Ronald McDonald as an international icon. . . .

One-Sided Critiques Miss Possible Benefits

Social scientists interested in consumption will be comfortable with . . . books [such as Schlosser's] for many reasons, not the least of which is the fact that they share the critical, even moralizing orientation, that dominates their work. I have no quarrel with this orientation; indeed I think that at least some good social scientific work should adopt such an approach—a 'debunking' of social myths. And there is no shortage of mythology associated with . . . McDonald's and [other cultural icons] which is greatly in need of debunking. However, within the academic literature on consumption a countertrend has emerged which focuses on a variety of positive aspects. Much work on consumption has been criticized for its relentless negativity, the tendency of its authors to adopt a god-like position that only they truly understand what they are observing, and a propensity to take an elitist view toward consumers who continue to consume and enjoy these products as well as adopting a positive, even reverential, view of the corporations which produce them. Academics are taking note of these criticisms and offering more balanced perspectives on consumption-related issues.

No such balance is to be found in . . . books [such as Schlosser's]. They are determinedly critical and have little to say of a positive nature about [their subjects]. In fact, this is one of the things that gives them their power and makes them attractive to a popular readership. A one-sided argument is of far greater force and interest than the more balanced treatments offered by most academics. In fact, a good case could be made that even within academic discourse we need more one-sided work like that found in [such] books. However, the fact is that such works, by their very nature, leave out many relevant issues, especially the positive side of the things they study. Let me enumerate of the arguments that could be made about the positive sides of the phenomena of concern in these [kinds of] books:

- the fast-food restaurant was made necessary by the movement of women into the labor force and the proliferation of such restaurants, and their clones in many other parts of the service sector have made it possible for many more women to enter the labor force. Were we to shutter all McDonaldized settings, many people (probably primarily women) would be forced back into the home.

- the fast-food restaurants offer consumers meals which are fast, convenient and predictable and which children like to eat.

Of course, this is just a sampling. Much more of a positive nature could and should be said of these phenomena and many other aspects of the consumer world. . . .

A McDonaldized World

One of the things that the reader of [such] books emerges with is a much greater sense of the increasing rapaciousness and rampant expansionism of contemporary capitalism. Within the United States, the contemporary move to the right initiated by [former president] Ronald Reagan (and now [in

Workers process beef at a meat packing plant in Wichita, Kansas, in 2004. © Ed Lallo/ ZUMA/Corbis.

2002] being carried forward by George W. Bush) has, among many other things, freed capitalists of many restraints. For example, . . . the Reagan administration initiated a policy of gutting anti-trust regulations and enforcement, thereby setting the stage for the giant mergers of the 1980s and 1990s and the creation of huge conglomerates that are more or less beyond the law. Outside the United States, the demise of Soviet communism and the transformation of at least the economy of China into one that is capitalistic, if not characterized by the worst excesses of capitalism, have eliminated any serious barrier to capitalistic expansion. The wide array of world trade agreements (including NAFTA: North American Free Trade Agreement) has served a similar end. (While . . . fast food restaurants and [other such consumer phenomena] all pre-date these developments, they were swept up in and given great impetus by them.)

Such changes have led, in turn, to many of the developments described by . . . Schlosser and [others], although they are not always clear about the root source of the phenomena they describe. The fast-food restaurant permits new levels of the exploitation of workers. For example, most workers are part time which means that they do not qualify for health insurance, pensions, and so on. As [Naomi Klein] describes [in her book *No Logo: Taking Aim at the Brand Name Bullies*], they can be kept on call and brought into work for a few hours as demand requires and then sent home when the demand slows. And the fast-food restaurant has been in the forefront of transforming customers into unpaid workers, at least for a few seconds or minutes of each visit. During this time they perform tasks (e.g. serving as waitpersons transporting their own food to their table, or as bus persons cleaning up after themselves) that, in the past, employees were paid to handle.

The latter involves a process whereby the fast-food chains have pushed not only McDonaldization, but exploitation, downward to workers and customers. Furthermore, as Schlosser points out, they have also pushed exploitation 'up' to those who supply them with the things they need to do business. Thus, Schlosser depicts the ways in which the requirements of the fast-food restaurant have forced those who raise and produce the food they need to increase their level of exploitation. The best example of this is in the meat-packing industry where the demands of the fast-food industry are responsible, at least in part, for the de-unionization of much of the industry, the hiring of low-paid workers (often illegal immigrants), and the speeding up of the production line to reduce costs (and increase profits). The result is inhuman work in inhumane conditions. Workers are reduced to fast-moving cogs in the assembly-line killing and butchering of animals. They are forced to perform repetitive and physically demanding tasks on animals that may, at least initially, not even be dead. They are often covered in blood and forced to stand in pools of blood. They wield very sharp knives at great speed in close proximity to other workers. The result is an extraordinarily high injury (and even death) rate although many

injuries go unreported out of fear of being fired for being injured and unable to perform at peak levels. The jobs are held
by non-unionized employees who are often immigrants (many
illegal). The result is that they are totally at the whim of a
management that is free to hire and fire them at will. Management is also enabled to ignore the horrid working conditions
confronted by these powerless employees, or to make them
even more horrific.

Exposé and Excess

Cecelia Tichi

Cecelia Tichi is William R. Kenan Jr. Professor of English at Vanderbilt University in Nashville, Tennessee.

With the separation of creative writing and journalism in universities, educators and critics may unfortunately dismiss Eric Schlosser's Fast Food Nation *as mere reportage. This is the core of Tichi's argument in the following viewpoint. Tichi believes the legacy of muckraking journalism and its precarious reception at the beginning of the twentieth century has unfairly pigeonholed all subsequent books that seek to expose the unfair or ruinous practices of American industry and keeps them from critical attention in academia. However, she maintains that* Fast Food Nation *and similar works present readers with issues that have also been addressed in books that are part of the literary canon. In addition, because Schlosser's claims that the fast food industry model has been impacting other aspects of society—including academia—Tichi suggests that literary educators have a vested interest in approaching these narratives with more respect and care.*

Eric Schlosser's best-selling *Fast Food Nation: The Dark Side of the All-American Meal*, narratively maps the post–World War II demographic pattern of US food production, interstate highways, and ubiquitous fast-food outlets from McDonald's to Subway and Taco Bell. Schlosser, a contributor to *Rolling Stone* and *The Atlantic Monthly* and a former student of the acclaimed nonfiction writer John Mcphee, exposes the treacherous working conditions and abysmal pay of meat-processing workers and the growing labor peonage of ranchers enfeoffed

Cecelia Tichi, "Exposé and Excess," *American Literary History*, vol. 15, no. 4, 2003, pp. 822–28. By permission of Oxford University Press. All rights reserved. Reproduced by permission.

to the meat-packing oligopoly. He juxtaposes individual entrepreneurship in the food industry to the incursions of corporate food and agribusiness into schools and other public places. Schlosser's is a narrative that is dense with facts, stylistically elegant, and narratively cunning.

The problematic position of *Fast Food Nation* and complementary texts in literary studies, however, can be traced to its generic lineage. Because Schlosser's book describes dire c. 2000 meat-processing conditions (call it Charlie Chaplin's *Modern Times* meets Hieronymus Bosch), it invites comparison to *The Jungle* (1906). It links itself, thereby, to the narrative tradition of early-twentieth-century writers who called theirs a literature of exposé or disclosure. These writers— including Ray Stannard Baker, Lincoln Steffens, and Ida M. Tarbell—lost the naming rights to their projects when, in 1906, President Theodore Roosevelt dubbed them muckrakers. Modifying an image from John Bunyan's *Pilgrims Progress*, Roosevelt acknowledged the prevalent "filth" of corruption in business and public life in the US and asserted the need to remove it with a Bunyanesque "muck-rake." Warning, however, that those writers who relentlessly plied that rake threatened the social order and were agents of "evil," he arguably hobbled the cohort of literary social critics even as he named them.

US literary critical history has ignored or given this group short shrift for decades. They (together with their heirs, including Schlosser and a cohort of c. 2000 new muckrakers) were damned with faintest praise in Alfred Kazin's influential *On Native Grounds*. Kazin judged the movement in terms reminiscent of natural disaster: "[S]uddenly released in a flood," the American "native grounds" were inundated when a collective mental dam broke. The muckraking movement, said Kazin, was one raging intellectual and emotional tumult. Segue to Van Wyck Brooks's *The Confident Years: 1885–1915* and we find the movement characterized in Cold War terms of alien invasion and infection festering in the body politic. Brooks understood the muckrakers to be acolytes of Russian immigrant anarchists still fighting the tyranny of czarist Russia in Manhattan's lower East side.

Post-1940s–1950s literary critical practices further eclipsed the muckrakers because New Criticism favored literary forms hostile to the muckrakers' own. Against a critical regimen of knowledge pursued through the interpretation of distinct linguistic features, principally metaphor and symbol, the muckrakers' ethos of discursive transparency appeared unliterary and thus unworthy of critical attention. (In this sense, Brooks's barb about muckrakers' "superficialities" struck true even as he turned their salient and carefully honed feature—accessibility—against them.) In the interdisciplinary field of American studies, meanwhile, the muckrakers fared no better because New Criticism made itself felt in the myth-and-symbol school, which argued that societal conflict could be codified in complex cultural symbols such as machines, gardens, and public figures, notably Charles Lindbergh or Andrew Jackson. No muckraker text was plumbed for its cultural symbol, nor for its divers types of ambiguity à la William Empson's landmark New Critical *Seven Types of Ambiguity* (1966).

The division between two categories—"literature" and "journalism"—further suppressed revaluation of the muckrakers. From the long-standing literary studies standpoint, these writers are *merely* journalists. The literary critic, both in and out of the academy, has the higher calling, in the true meaning of vocation (from the Latin *vocare*). The journalist, on the other hand, is merely a Voc-Ed worker. (Programs in journalism and in English typically exist in separate academic departments, schools, or university colleges, an arrangement normalized over decades, with writers designated as "creative" separated from those in journalistic "training.")

The inclusion of *Fast Food Nation* in literary studies (along with new muckraker texts of c. 2000, such as Barbara

Ehrenreich's *Nickel and Dimed: On (Not) Getting By in America* and Naomi Klein's *No Logo: Taking Aim at the Brand Bullies*) thus requires an analysis of texts according to different criteria, most promisingly those of narrative studies. Of practical value here are the work of Peter Brooks on plot and melodrama, the discussion by Hayden White of truth claims, and the argument of James Phelan on narrative design and the use of facts. According to Christopher Nash, a theorist of narrative, muckraker narratives arguably open themselves to the kind of "radical writing" that "claims to strike at the root (social, for example) of things 'outside' the text"—which is to say, narrative able to intercede directly in the sociopolitical realm.

The notion of Schlosser as reprise of Upton Sinclair nonetheless prompts distinctions across a century. In *The Jungle*, for instance, the main characters, Lithuanian immigrants, are all downtrodden workers whose bosses are purebred villains. *Fast Food Nation*, on the other hand, widens the spectrum of its dramatis personae by featuring several compelling and sympathetic biographies of self-made American entrepreneurs, such as John Richard Simplot, a onetime Idaho potato farmer who became one of America's richest men through a potato empire supplying the military and McDonald's. (Simplot's is the name responsible for the crispy golden arch fries.)

Other differences are equally salient. In *The Jungle*, Sinclair made the cri de coeur of the Chicago packinghouse worker the metaphoric "hog squeal of the universe." Sinclair's metaphor exploits his audience's assenting familiarity with the sensational tradition of nineteenth-century sentimental-melodramatic narrative. Its decibel level is high, its appeal to emotion direct and intense.

In 2001, in contrast, *Fast Food Nation* deploys an aesthetic image of slaughterhouse "Whizzards peeling meat off decapitated heads [of cattle], picking them almost as clean as the white skulls painted by Georgia O'Keeffe." Schlosser, like Sinclair, presents a slaughterhouse that is alien to bourgeois readers. Schlosser's art image, however, avoids such techniques of nineteenth-century sensationalism. His antiphony of narrative and metaphor works within an interpretive framework of emotional containment. It operates in accord with an understated narrative style typified by his former teacher, McPhee. It stabilizes the horrific for a reading community whose class identity is affirmed by reference to exhibition spectatorship of art. The reference to O'Keeffe signals a narrator who construes his readers as late-twentieth-century art devotees aware of metropolitan museum showings, such as the Georgia O'Keeffe multicity exhibit of the late 1980s (with ancillary gift-shop reproductions, coffee table books, and documentary TV footage). Each narrative, Sinclair's and Schlosser's, rhetorically shapes, and is shaped by, the reading community it serves.

The reception of *Fast Food Nation*, however, reveals the challenge of investigative narrative in its relation to the reading public(s) of varying class status, gender, and ethnoracial identities. A major issue in Schlosser, to take one case in point, concerns contemporary workplace conditions in the meat-packing industry, a topic that is framed in telling detail: "[T]he voices and faces of these workers are indelibly with me, as is the sight of their hands, the light brown skin criss-crossed with white scars." Schlosser characterizes one loyal packing-house worker, Kenny, whose body, from his skeletal-muscular system to his immune system, his respiratory system, and his heart, is permanently damaged by work-related injuries that tally the careless indifference of his employer, the Monfort company, which has fired him. Totally disabled and destitute in his mid-forties, Kenny says, "They used me to the point where I had no body parts to give." Schlosser's narrative voice maintains its understated dispassion: "His anger at Monfort, his feelings of betrayal, are of truly biblical proportions." Readers of *Fast Food Nation* are thus reminded of Schlosser's stated fact, that the death and injury rates of packinghouse workers are the highest of any occupational group, making packinghouses the most dangerous workplaces in America.

However, public response to *Fast Food Nation* has largely ignored the topic of workplace conditions, whether in the packing plants or nationwide in the fast-food industry in which employees earn the minimum hourly wage without health care or other benefits. These workers, so prominent in *Fast Food Nation*, are the "disappeareds" in the glowing excerpts from 39 reviews that preface the 2002 paperback edition. The blurbs praise Schlosser's narrative skill, his exhaustive research into every area of the topic, his wit and "flair for dazzling scene-setting and an arsenal of startling facts," as the *Los Angeles Times* put it.

Only 3 of the 39 reviewers, however, name working conditions as significant in Schlosser's project. "This is a book about America's stomach," according to the *Baltimore Sun*, and thus does reader response make *Fast Food Nation* another *The Jungle* in recalling Upton Sinclair's wry remark that he had aimed for the public's heart and hit the stomach instead. Schlosser's own observation on the post-1960s disappearance of the working middle class in part explains why the workers' stories have received scant attention in reviews of *Fast Food Nation*. Yet reading practices in the academy in the latter half of the twentieth century may have a significant role in shaping such critical response. Academic reading practices are arguably complicitous with a normalization of class division that effectively effaces non-elites.

Suppose, for instance, that some of Schlosser's reviewers, like many of his readers, have studied a certain well-known narrative combining the slaughterhouse and its workers. *Moby-Dick* features several chapters on whale slaughter and butchering, as Melville invites readers to consider the terms of their own red meat diets—the "meat-market of a Saturday night," the "gourmand dining off that roast beef," the mate Stubb's delectable dinner of grilled whale steak.

An illustration by A. Burnham Shute for Herman Melville's nineteenth-century novel Moby Dick, *about the treacherous whaling industry.* © Bettmann/Corbis.

Melville precedes Schlosser by one and a half centuries, but he, too, had specified the danger and risk of the slaughtering-butchering work of whale oil production for lighting and lubrication in the pre-petroleum era. For instance, the thin hemp whale-line, which is tied to the harpoon to be thrust into the unsuspecting whale, must be coiled in perfect "minute spiralizations" free of any tangle or kink. Failure to take this "utmost precaution" can mean the loss of a crewman's arm, leg, or "entire body" when the harpooned whale dives deep.

A second line from an additional whale boat is sometimes needed, the second boat hovering nearby "to assist its consort," lest the first boat "be dragged down . . . into the profundity of the sea," that is, "doomed." "This arrangement," says Melville, "is indispensable for common safety's sake." The work is terribly dangerous, the pitching boat more perilous than the comparable earthly industrial scene of "manifold whizzings of a steam-engine in full play, when every flying beam, and shaft, and wheel, is grazing you." For mutual self-protection, however, the crew follow safety procedures, which Melville specifies in detail.

Have classroom teachers of American literature asked students to pay attention to working conditions on this factory ship, the *Pequod*, and thereby helped educate students—future book reviewers and readers—about the importance of the topic in their civic lives? In the last 20 years, as the workplace safety protections mandated in union contracts (and middle-class pay scales) disappeared, have we resorted to this American classic to frame classroom discussions of the workplace in canonical American literature?

No. We leap eagerly, instead, to Melville's philosophical musing that "all men live enveloped in whale-lines," that "all are born with halters round their necks" and realize the "silent, subtle, ever-present perils of life" only when "caught in the swift, sudden turn of death." These are the phrases underscored in our classroom desk copies, these the metaphysical statements we call to students' attention. These, we emphasize, are the so-called enduring truths, or conundrums of the human condition worldwide across millennia. Perhaps, additionally, we might link these statements to the act of writing itself and claim that Melville was meditating on his own literary peril. Or we venture a psychoanalytic suggestion of birth crisis as the umbilical lifeline becomes death's noose.

None of these approaches, however, focuses on labor, its risks, the protocols for "common safety's sake." None, that is, encourages civic obligation to take legislative responsibility for worksite conditions. They appeal instead to a community of readers predisposed to expect a high-minded "classic" text, classicism itself understood to exclude direct social engagement. After all, our college and university students are not and never will be slaughterhouse or long-term fast-food workers.

Five years following the publication of *The Jungle*, the American Academy of Political and Social Science published a volume entitled *Risks in Modern Industry* (1911). It is a compilation of statements by a wide range of officials voicing differing viewpoints on a topic that all participants agreed needed urgent attention in the US: the high rates of industrial-era injury and death of workers. The Secretary of Commerce and Labor weighed in, as did a consulting engineer, a vice president of the American Federation of Labor, an assistant district attorney of New York, a Unitarian minister, a member of the executive committee of the American Red Cross, and the General Secretary of the National Consumers' League.

Given their positions, their statements were to some degree predictable. The Secretary of Commerce and Labor voiced the business goal to minimize waste with a minimum of governmental regulation, while the labor union leader promoted workers' health. The district attorney emphasized mutual responsibility of management and workers for meeting provisions of the new worker compensation law in his state, New York, while the Red Cross spokeswoman highlighted the need to prevent workplace disasters.

The pages of Risks in Modern Industry, however, are rife with convergent statements on "accidents . . . out of proportion," on "the number of men and women annually killed and maimed in the industrial occupations of America . . . [being] greater than in the bloodiest battles of history," on victims' "dependents who suffer the direct and terrible consequences of the family of a wage earner . . . carried lifeless into his home." They speak of the "enormous" social and economic costs, of the new possibility for "elementary justice," and of the fact that the very term disaster refers not only to "pestilence, famine, fire, and floods" but also to the "calamity" of industrial accidents in which a half-million people are estimated to be annually killed or injured in the US.

Slaughterhouse workers were not singled out for attention in the 1911 volume, nor in its 1926 successor, Industrial Safety, whose title accentuated the gains made over 15 years in worker protection via an organized safety movement. Heavy industry—notably steel, coal, and railroads—took precedence, and no food-processing industry was named. The trend toward worker protection, however, was clear. A fast-food nation was then decades in the offing, as was the rise—and subsequent decline—of unionized work in the US. As Schlosser states toward the close of Fast Food Nation. "Over the past twenty-five years the United States has swung too far in one direction, weakening the regulations that safeguard workers, consumers, and the environment. An economic system promising freedom has too often become a means of denying it, as the narrow dictates of the market gain precedence over more important democratic values."

Workplace conditions in the downsizing era of the second, c. 2000, Gilded Age, however, may tend to aggregate workers, if not into a uniform collar, at least into proximity and mutual regard. The individual workers in *Fast Food Nation*, Schlosser argues, typify groups "linked by common elements" that prove to be common not only to blue-collar workers but also to those in high-rise towers and office parks and even college and university campuses—"the same struggle to receive proper medical care, the same fear of speaking out, the same underlying corporate indifference." Those at the desk may come to see kindred spirits, or at least distant relations, across the fast-food counter and over the computer keyboard to the boning knife. Classroom reading practices can change, and the American literature syllabus can diversify to include a literature of exposé and disclosure. "There is nothing inevitable about the fast food nation that surrounds us," as Schlosser writes in his afterword to the 2002 paperback edition. "Things don't have to be the way they are."

Works Cited

American Academy of Political and Social Science. *Risks in Modern Industry*. Philadelphia: American Academy of Political and Social Science, 1911.

Brooks, Van Wyck. *The Confident Years: 1885–1915*. New York: Dutton, 1952.

Kazin, Alfred. *On Native Grounds: An Interpretation of Modern American Prose Literature*. New York: Reynal and Hitchcock, 1942.

Melville, Herman. *Moby-Dick; or, The Whale*. 1851. New York: Penguin, 1986.

Nash, Christopher. "Slaughtering the Subject: Literature's Assault on Narrative." *Narrative in Culture*. Ed. Christopher Nash. New York: Routledge, 1990. 199–218.

Roosevelt, Theodore. "The Man with the Muck-rake." 1906. Rpt. in *The Treason of the Senate* by David Graham Phillips. Ed. George E. Mowry and Judson A. Grenier. New York: Quadrangle, 1964.

Schlosser, Eric. Afterword, *Fast Food Nation: The Dark Side of th All-American Meal.* Pbk. ed. New York: HarperCollins, 2002. 171–88.

Sinclair, Upton. *The Jungle.* 1906. New York: Penguin, 1985.

Fast Food Nation Has Encouraged Consumers to Take Action Against the Fast Food Industry

Andrew Engelson

Andrew Engelson is the former editor of Washington Trails *magazine and continues to write and blog at www.onlyok.net.*

In the following viewpoint, Engelson discusses an interview he had with Eric Schlosser about Schlosser's book Fast Food Nation. *Engelson speaks of the dangers of the fast food industry that Schlosser enumerates, but he also mentions that the only successful reform of these hazards have been brought about by consumers. Engelson states that* Fast Food Nation *convinced him to stop eating fast food, and he expects that reaction may spread and encourage other consumers to stand up for better product and more socially conscious business practices within the industry.*

In the year since the publication of Eric Schlosser's *Fast Food Nation* [in 2001], more than a few readers have given up putting Quarter Pounders and other fast food into their mouths. You can add this reader to that list. I'll admit, it's going to be tough. I have a severe weakness for McNuggets.

But the facts presented in *Fast Food Nation* make it clear that companies like McDonald's need to literally clean up their acts before this consumer eats fast food again.

Schlosser's muckraking exposé of the fast-food and meat-packing industries was one of 2001's surprise best sellers. Recently published in paperback, the book now has the potential

Andrew Engelson, "What's Eating This Guy? The Fast-Food Industry," *The Seattle Post-Intelligencer*, January 17, 2002. Andrew Engleson/Seattlepi.com. Reproduced by permission.

to alert even more readers to the hidden costs of what at first glance appears to be cheap fast food.

I recently spoke with Schlosser, an investigative reporter for the *Atlantic* magazine, before his first visit to the Seattle area to promote the book. Whether he's citing statistics or describing conditions in meatpacking plants, Schlosser is a quietly passionate critic of an industry many of us take for granted.

The Dangers and Costs

"Fast food has been unbelievably successful in the United States," he said. "It has transformed what we eat and how food is produced. And it's been increasingly successful overseas, particularly in the United Kingdom, in Japan and in Germany. McDonald's is now the biggest purchaser of agricultural products in France and the biggest private employer in Brazil."

According to another of the many factoids that flavor Schlosser's book, Americans spend more on fast food than they do on movies, books, magazines, newspapers, videos and recorded music combined.

Fast Food Nation reveals that despite its successes, this enormous industry has imposed an array of hidden costs on the U.S. economy: the proliferation of minimum-wage, low-skill jobs, the consolidation of the meatpacking industry in to the hands of a few extremely powerful corporations, the dramatic increase in rates of obesity, the homogenization of American neighborhoods with identical fast-food restaurants, the growth of marketing to children and increasingly dangerous working conditions in meatpacking plants.

It's this last point that Schlosser is perhaps most emotional about. "Meatpacking used to be one of the highest-paid industrial jobs in the United States," he said. "It was like being an autoworker. While it wasn't an easy job, you could have a decent middle-class life. Today it is one of the lowest-paid in-

Demonstrating continued worldwide demand for fast food, patrons flock to eat Big Macs discounted in celebration of the twentieth anniversary of the McDonald's in downtown Budapest, Hungary, in 2008. © Attila Kisbenedek/AFP/Getty Images.

dustrial jobs in the United States, and it has one of the highest turnover rates of any industry."

His book provides a stark picture of modern meatpacking plants and the bleak towns that have sprung up around them. During his upcoming visit to the Northwest, Schlosser plans to visit a union meeting to discuss injury rates among workers at an IBP [Iowa Beef Processors, Inc.] meatpacking plant in Pasco. IBP is the nation's largest producer of ground beef, and frequent target in Schlosser's book for its practices of recruiting immigrant labor, breaking unions and allowing dangerous conditions to exist in its plants.

Only Consumers Can Create Change

Schlosser thinks increased pressure by consumers can help increase safety standards in these plants. He points to a recent campaign by People for the Ethical Treatment of Animals [PETA] that succeeded in pressuring McDonald's suppliers to treat animals humanely.

"McDonald's did the right thing," said Schlosser. "They issued a tough set of guidelines for the ethical treatment of animals in slaughterhouses that supply them. I think they now need to do the same for human beings who work these slaughterhouses and make sure they're also being treated humanely."

Despite all of these social costs, one issue seems to stand out. It's the most personal and visceral: the prevalence of pathogens in ground beef. Though he's not a vegetarian, Schlosser has sworn off ground beef until things change.

"Fast food has transformed our agriculture system and industrialized it. You have a centralized system that can spread bad bugs far and wide very quickly. Right now, as we speak, it is perfectly legal in the United States to sell ground beef totally tainted with salmonella, and the government can't do anything about it," he said, referring to a recent federal court ruling that prevents the Department of Agriculture from shutting down beef plants because of salmonella contamination.

Schlosser is quick to note that fast-food companies have independently instituted tough new inspection standards in the wake of E. coli deaths that struck customers of Jack in the Box restaurants in the early 1990s. But industrial agriculture companies, which the fast-food industry helped create, continue to oppose new government regulation. As a result, tainted meat makes its way into supermarkets, schools and American homes.

"Over a million people are hospitalized for salmonella each year, and this costs several thousand dollars per person," said Schlosser. "Maybe people would be willing to pay literally pennies more for their hamburger to make sure the meat is properly tested and isn't going to make them sick."

Schlosser is a talented writer, and his book makes for compulsive reading. In addition to profiling the industry's abuses, he examines the fascinating history of fast food. "The early part of this industry is a great American story," he said.

"It only gets dark when it gets too big and powerful and disconnected from ordinary human values."

Until they reconnect, there will be no McNuggets for this reader.

Fast Food Nation Helps Students Become More Aware of Their Food Choices

Madhu Suri Prakash and Dana L. Stuchul

Madhu Suri Prakash is a professor of education at Pennsylvania State University, and Dana L. Stuchul is associate professor of education in the Department of Curriculum and Instruction at the same university.

In the following viewpoint, Prakash and Stuchul argue that Eric Schlosser's Fast Food Nation *is an excellent educational tool to get students thinking about the choices they make in a world that is shaped by the fast food industry and its propensity for speed. Prakash and Stuchul maintain that the book opens students' eyes to the hidden hazards and risks of the industry, but, more significantly, it forces them to consider how that industry has created winners and losers in society and generated a lifestyle in America that encourages conformity, consumption, and ignorance of the social and physical environments. The authors believe* Fast Food Nation *can galvanize students to explore alternatives to this fast-paced, rapacious lifestyle and bring about personal and social change.*

Serendipitously, a surprise encounter with a student in the neighborhood park brought the genius of Eric Schlosser's *Fast Food Nation* into our hands two years ago. Given your goals of environmental education, she mused, connecting food for thought with food for the belly, you will find rich reflections in *Fast Food Nation.* Our students constantly enrich our

Madhu Suri Prakash and Dana L. Stuchul, "Fast Food and Environmental Awareness," *Encounter*, vol. 16, no. 4, Winter 2003, pp. 49–54. Copyright © 2003 Psychology Press/
Holistic Education Press. All rights reserved. Reproduced by permission.

curricula and pedagogy. Once again our students became our teacher. Soon after, the book became central to our philosophy of education course for undergraduate education majors.

In our university [Pennsylvania State University], one cannot help but feel compassion for the undergraduates crammed into classrooms, moved through programs, and then finally processed into professionals. In swift, orderly, indistinguishable fashion, students progress toward their places within society. They dash from dorm to dining hall, apartment to eatery, meeting groups, navigating libraries, submitting papers and projects all for the goal of matriculation. Their lives are fast. And speed, for all of its allure, exacts a price.

Students Often Eat Fast Food

Fast food feels like no fad for our students. To them it's a basic necessity. Many students declare that they would not eat if it were not the free home-delivery or the under five minute drive-in deal that liberates them from shopping, chopping, cooking, cleaning, mopping . . . and disposing of the black garbage bag at the curbside.

For Laura, it's a matter of simple pride in her single mother who could raise her whole brood, abandoned by their father, thanks to the meal deals wheeled out by the fastest familiar eateries in her ghetto. For the majority, it's the freedom found to study and graduate faster on the already fast lane to graduation and a real job. For Debbie, who already has a real job, it's her savior. This underpaid teacher struggling with advanced certification in our summer intensive course, is raising her own three kids alone, while seeking to motivate and inspire the 23 children in her fifth grade class.

So go the stories of Week 1 of our course. The celebration of fast food is unabashed.

Schlosser's stories bring to life for them the American dream turned fabulous reality by Ray Kroc, one of the founding fathers of McDonalds, or of Carl Karcher, Richard and

Maurice "Mac" Donald, Harland Sanders, and the other emperors of the fast food empire. With the raw guts and tenacity admired in the pioneers opening new frontiers, they brought about the "industrial eating" revolution that revolutionized the lives of millions across the nation; and now promises to do so across the world's "global economy." A revolution started without arms and ammunition, the victorious golden arches rise over highways as the universally famous, luminous "mother McDonald's breasts." Our students love Schlosser's stories of "rags to riches" that keep alive, for them, the American Dream.

Teaching About the Impact of Fast Food

When beginning to explore the connection between fast food and philosophy of education, here's what the bravest and boldest students are provoked to ask: "Professors, we know all about fast food. We eat it every day. What does fast food for the belly have to do with food for thought? What does *Fast Food Nation* have to do with education?"

To begin addressing these questions, students learn not only of the enormity of the fast food industry (Americans spend more on fast food than higher education, computers, or new cars), but how the industry reflects and permeates the society.

Schlosser compels students to pause—perhaps for the first time in their lives—before their beloved nation's fast food economy. As they discover in the chapter, "Why the Fries Taste So Good," the picture of a sophisticated scientific and technological achievement emerges. Fries taste good not because of the potato or grease but because of a myriad of flavor and aroma compounds added to ensure uniformity of both. With this revelation, our students begin to re-evaluate their taken-for-granted understanding of what's in the "food"? What exactly is "food," anyway? Real food? Fossil fuels and other chemicals?

Schlosser's answers take us behind the fast food counter, into the factory, the trailer home, the field, the slaughterhouse and corporate headquarters. In his stories, our young eaters/ teachers-in-the-making smell and see the real lives of adolescents sickened by "affluenza." Slowly, ever so slowly, the picture emerges of the penetration of a fast food ethos and reality into their schools, into contemporary classrooms, athletic fields, school buses, and not the least, cafeterias—alluring young eaters and image targets, even as they contradict lessons learned in health class, science class, and social studies class. But it is still some time before the answer to the question of what all of this has to do with education and the philosophy of education comes into focus.

Schlosser takes his readers a part of the long way [writer and agricultural activist] Wendell Berry has traveled to discover:

> It would not do for the consumer to know that the hamburger she is eating came from a steer who spent much of his life standing deep in his own excrement in a feedlot, helping to pollute the local streams, or that the calf that yielded the veal cutlet on her plate spent its life in a box in which it did not have room to turn around. And, though her sympathy for the slaw might be less tender, she should not be encouraged to meditate on the hygienic and biological implications of mile-square fields of cabbage, for vegetables grown in huge monocultures are dependent on toxic chemicals—just as animals in close confinement are dependent on antibiotics and other drugs. . . . The industrial farm is said to have been patterned on the factory production line. In practice, it looks more like a concentration camp.

Life Lived at Fast Food Pace

Junk food junkies are fast fed into obliviousness—the grease-ease drug and admen's images convincing them that the "happy meal" spreads happiness across the global landscape. Schlosser's shake-up, however rudely felt at first, is finally seen as pertinent. Compassion for the eater and the eaten, for the fryer and the fried, for the farmer and the rancher rips through the lies, deceit, and conceit that feed all of us fast food. Students resonate with this compassion, even as they listen to the simple though disturbing facts revealed by Schlosser's well-documented research.

Students read how soils of small farms, community commons, and slow food villages are mauled and hauled away; laid over with concrete slabs of interstates working 24 hours a day to keep us addicted to the fast food that fuels our fast, thoughtless, crazy, stressed, damaged and damaging lives.

Schlosser's "speed bump" slows our students down, enabling them to consider the price paid in speeding. They recognize the stress speed bears, the stress that kills. Documenting tragedies behind the scenes, Schlosser reminds us that the suicide rate among ranchers and farmers in the United States is now about three times higher than the national average. Urging his readers to look beyond the immediate horror—the suicides and dismemberments destroying millions of families today—there is the future growing increasingly bleak and dark. Schlosser will not let us easily forget that in

> ranching, a failure is much more likely to be final. The land that has been lost is not just a commodity. It has meaning that cannot be measured in dollars and cents. It is a tangible connection with the past, something that was meant to be handed down to children and never sold.

For the founding fathers of fast food, such sentiments are meaningless. Their success as much as their candid words teach us the price that must be paid for the success that defines the American dream. Ray Kroc reminds us about the pillars of competition that undergird this economic philosophy. Free of all illusions of political correctness that his CEOs [chief executive officers] today must mouth, in plain language Kroc dismisses any high-minded analysis of fast food success:

"This is rat eat rat, dog eat dog. I'll kill 'em, and I'm going to kill 'em before they kill me. You're talking about the American way of survival of the fittest."

An Hourglass Economy

Describing the survival of the fittest in the food economy, Schlosser quotes [writer] William Heffernan who explains why the American agricultural economy now resembles an hourglass. "At the top there are about 2 million ranchers and farmers: at the bottom there are 275 million consumers; and at the narrow portion in the middle, there are a dozen or so multinational corporations earning a profit from every transaction."

> Over the past 25 years, Idaho has lost about half of its potato farmers. . . . Family farms are giving way to corporate farms that stretch for thousands of acres. You increasingly find two classes of people in rural Idaho: the people who run the farms and the people who own them.

Winners within the American hourglass oligopsony [a skewed market in which a small number of buyers controls a product or service], J.R. Simplot the potato farm tycoon being one, are not self-conscious in declaring: I have been a "land hog all my life." Simplot flies a gigantic American flag on a pole that's ten stories high and "controls a bloc of North American land that's bigger than the state of Delaware."

Schlosser celebrates the fast food success of specific moguls and emperors without glossing over the death of democracy that attends it. His prose creates openings for conversations with industrial eaters now conscious of the consequences of their eating addictions. "Strategic questioning" about the issue of democracy as personal action and commitment now becomes possible.

Slow Food Revolutions

In what can we place our hope, ask our students? "What can we do?"

Radical hope is the essence of popular movements, we remind our students and ourselves. Grassroots initiatives and movements are surging with hope from the ground up; hope that common people can escape the global economy's American-style, anti-democratic, oligopsonic eating hourglass. These common people seek to create new food commons; to regenerate democratic ways of eating; to re-birth their own cultural conceptions of democracy.

Taking us into the bowels of the beast, into the furthest reaches of the belly of the fast food empire, Schlosser offers stones of hope, courage, daring, and escape from "McDollars, McGreed, McCancer, McMurder, McProfits, McGarbage." Expressing the kind of immediate hope that our students can closely identify with, Schlosser's common sense suggests that

> Nobody in the United States is forced to buy fast food. The first step toward meaningful change is by far the easiest: stop buying it. . . . The heads of Burger King, KFC, and McDonald's should feel daunted; they're outnumbered. There are three of them and almost three hundred million of you. A good boycott, a refusal to buy, can speak much louder than words. Sometimes the most irresistible force is the most mundane.

Among the gutsy, gumption-filled Schlosser stories of today's Davids taking on Fast Food Goliaths, is the story of Helen Steel and Dave Morris; it is a marvelous moral tale of ordinary English people now resisting the domination of their lives by the Americanization of the world. Despite a vast international army of spies and attorneys deployed by the McDonald "Goliath," two school dropouts in Britain turned on its head the "McLibel" case[1] launched against them by McDonald's Corporation and won "the longest trial in British history," while creating a "public relations disaster for McDonald's."

1. Steel and Morris were sued for distributing a pamphlet in the mid-1980s entitled "What's Wrong with McDonald's: Everything They Don't Want You to Know."

If eaters like Helen Steel and Dave Morris are concerned about the contamination of their bellies, their mouths, and intestinal tracts with fast food poisons, then even more compelling are the tales of moral resistance coming from farmers whose way of working and life, of centuries-old family traditions are under brutal, bloody attack from "McGreed." Jose Bove, a French sheep farmer, demolished a McDonald's under construction in Millau, his hometown. "Lousy food" resister turned author of the bestseller *The World Is Not for Sale—and Nor Am I!*, this national hero risked even imprisonment while inviting his countrymen not to become "servile slaves at the service of agribusiness;" declaring, instead, "*non a McMerde* ['No to McSh-t']."

On this side of the Atlantic, south of the U.S. border, in the historic central plaza of Mexico's gracious Oaxaca, indigenous corn *tamales* won the day as thousands from all walks of life—from peasants and local restaurateurs to international intellectuals and world-renowned Mexican artists—came together to throw McDonald's out of its preferred and prestigious location in the historic central town plaza.

Schlosser shows that change—real, meaningful, life-sustaining change—is neither far away nor hard to achieve. It is as close to us as our own hands and mouths. Millions are waking up from speedy somnambulance.

Pushing for Social Change

Hope is further found in the fifty million "cultural creatives" now currently departing on diverse, unique, personal, innovative paths (or escape routes?) from their consumptive, ecologically destructive, speedy, stressful, unhealthy, anxiety-ridden, fast paced North American lives. They are creating what some are calling "The New American Dream." There is nothing flaky or New Age about this, writes Sarah van Gelder [in a 2001 issue of *Yes!*] "These people are practical. They love the Earth, and they want to live their values." They are, in the words of Joanna Macy [in her 1998 book *Coming Back to Life*] contributing to the "Great Turning."

In our course, we also include numerous accounts of hope-filled initiatives around the world and around the country. Daily, we celebrate in class teachers who take their students out of doors and engage their communities, and teachers who are not bound and gagged by state-mandated curricula or pre-packaged teaching materials. Our students come alive with hope upon learning that school yards across the country that were concreted over are being de-concreted; the soil set free after years of imprisonment—to breathe again; to grow green; to nourish and be nourished with food for the body, food for the mind and food for the soul/spirit.

If such stories from schools—elementary, middle and high—do not inspire enough confidence in student-teachers daunted by supposed superintendents demanding they teach to the standards-based tests, there is yet more abundant hope-filled food for inspiration. We need only proceed as far as our own state of Pennsylvania, where initiatives such as STREAMS (Science Teams in Rural Environments for Aquatic Management Studies) reveal how middle grades students involved in integrated and environment-based studies are outperforming their peers in traditional classrooms on standardized tests.

Spreading Ecological Awareness

Ostensibly, our work with undergraduate education majors attempts to marry studies in philosophy of education to ecological literacy. We do this because we want our students to be able to critically address issues relevant to the survival of places, peoples, ways of knowing; and to be better able to confront environmental matters of concern within their community, municipality, home, and neighborhood. Over and over, we are surprised by the number of students who are neither familiar with nor conversant in a whole host of environmental issues. We take seriously [author David] Orr's dictum [in his 1992 book *Ecological Literacy*] that "All education is environmental education." By omitting environmental studies from our philosophy of education courses, we would, in effect, be teaching that the environment is irrelevant to an examination of philosophical issues.

We seek to draw connections between environmental awareness and students' answers to questions such as What is the good life? What is happiness?, and What does it mean to be educated? Forgoing the common approach to philosophical studies, we instead use environmental studies as the arena in which to provoke our students to ask what is education? And what is education for?

[In his 1975 book *Moral Principles in Education*, philosophy professor John] Dewey long ago concluded that "the subject-matter of the curriculum, however important, however judiciously selected, is empty of conclusive moral content until it is made over into terms ot the individual's own activities, habits, and desires."

In our use of Schlosser's *Fast Food Nation*, our intention is to align our pedagogy with Deweyan philosophy, to begin with our students' activities, habits, and desires. The "speed bump" that is *Fast Food Nation* is so effective among undergraduates primarily due to their familiarity with fast food. As former employees, they recognize the working conditions— late hours, surprising job responsibilities, and low wages— detailed by Schlosser. As former children, they speak fondly of toys, prizes, and playgrounds, all memories of serene, uncomplicated, joyous bygone days. As adolescents, they express gratitude for the convenience of warm food given the demands of school and extracurricular activities on shared family time. And, today as students busily preparing for their future vocation as educators, the irony of fast food as the one pause in lives lived fast is not lost on them.

Making Ecological Literacy Approachable

What is revealed to them are the effects of speed on landscapes, familial relationships, civic participation, wealth distribution, health, and community life. They begin to see the consequent fragmentation of living within their fast food nation: of knowing from doing, of schooling from community, of individuals from democratic action, of knowledge itself, and of living from the environment. So begins the opening to environmental awareness. So begins an approach to an answer to the question, "What does fast food have to do with education?"

Schlosser's *Fast Food Nation* admirably shows us how we can slow ourselves down to even consider the price paid in speeding. *Fast Food Nation*, wedded to environmental awareness, yields a match made in heaven for bringing ecological literacy down to earth from distant ozone holes to the immediacy of what we put into our mouths several times every day.

Our students report that because of *Fast Food Nation*, their eyes are "open to things never thought of before . . . making me want to make changes in my life and education and in others so that they can also make changes if they choose to." They report new insights about what is going on behind the scenes and in rural towns. They speak about their new interests in "knowing where your food comes from and what's in it" and of their wish to have read these stories and facts years earlier. To our delight, they share course materials with roommates, talk about it with parents, and opt not to sell *Fast Food Nation* and other course texts back to the bookstore at the end of the term! They swear off fast food, considering how they might, despite the restrictions of budget and time, incorporate food that is slow rather than fast into their lives; local, regional, and seasonal rather than that which travels long, international distances; food that supports rootedness and a sense of place rather than uprootedness, destruction, and thoughtlessness.

Once their food and all of its costs (ecological, social, or moral) have been accounted for, our students are now open to consider how their education has been similarly divorced from soil, landscapes, and environment. They begin to critically consider the previously unquestioned pedagogies to which they themselves have been subjected, pedagogies that have rendered them passive, uncritical, and unknowledgeable about innumerable concrete realities, not the least of which is their food and their relationship to places. Soon they begin to request participation in initiatives within the community as part of the class—from food banks and CSA [community supported agriculture] farm distribution to educational events (children's activities at Earth Day celebrations, summer camps, and enrichment programs offered to visiting high school students). They begin to cook together, inviting classmates to potlucks made of foods purchased and grown locally. Some even take to gardening.

Beyond the Standard Curriculum

Seeing gaps in their own knowledge about food as revealed in *Fast Food Nation*, they begin to recognize additional gaps in their knowledge that are equally critical to their own survival. From health practices to democracy, they see anew what is meant by "the hidden curriculum"; what they're not learning about the environment they soon recognize as akin to what they're not learning in other, equally essential areas. Soon, they take hold of their learning, no longer passive consumers. From pallet to intellect, stomach to mind, students begin to slow themselves, and in slowing answer the questions that will sustain them in all of the ways we seek sustenance.

In this slow mulling, they are liberated to accept the invitation [of Berry] to eat with the

> fullest pleasure—pleasure, that is, that does not depend on ignorance, perhaps the profoundest enactment of our connection with the world. In this pleasure we experience and

celebrate our dependence and our gratitude, for we are living from mystery, from creatures we did not make and powers we cannot comprehend.

Eric Schlosser's Writings on the Food Industry Obscure and Ignore the Facts

Steven C. Anderson

Steven C. Anderson is a former president and chief executive of the National Restaurant Association, an industry advocacy organization.

In the viewpoint that follows, Anderson takes issue with the reporting of facts and opinions in Eric Schlosser's Fast Food Nation *and* Chew on This. *Anderson argues that these attacks on the food industry provide misinformation that makes food service seem scary and uncaring. In reality, statistics reveal that employees in the food sector are safer than many other professions and have thrived in the business, earning good wages and proving their loyalty. Anderson also refutes Schlosser's claims that the food industry's products have led to a rise in childhood obesity in the United States. Anderson maintains that the industry is always seeking new ways to make its products safe and affordable for all consumers.*

Anti-restaurant activist Eric Schlosser has made a living promoting misinformation and misrepresentation—most notoriously with his *New York Times* best-selling book, *Fast Food Nation*. Previously Schlosser peddled propaganda to adults, and he now has written a children's book for those ages 9 to 12.

Titled *Chew On This*, his latest diatribe hits bookstores next month [in June 2006] and looks to be as full of what *The Wall Street Journal* called Schlosser's "cavalier manipulation of data" as previous efforts.

Steven C. Anderson, "The Best Defense Against Propaganda Is Good Information," *Nation's Restaurant News*, vol. 40, no. 19, May 8, 2006, pp.100–101. Copyright © 2006 by Gale, Cengage Learning. All rights reserved. Reproduced by permission.

Schlosser hopes teachers will use his book to persuade children to eliminate America's quick-service restaurants from future career and dining choices, making it critical that our industry is armed with the facts.

Countering Misinformation

Look, we all care about the issues Mr. Schlosser is raising. He might even have some credibility if nothing had ever been done to address these matters. But the reality of today's ever-growing, ever-better world of restaurant employment, ownership and customer service absolutely trumps his misguided views.

Take jobs. Schlosser wants to influence young people's thinking by branding restaurant jobs as "dead end." Yet the facts tell us that one in four Americans began their working lives in a restaurant, and nearly half of all adults have worked in the industry at some point during their careers.

In Schlosser's scary-sounding world, the "typical" foodservice employee is fired after three or four months. In reality, the typical foodservice employee remains on the job for close to one and a half years, and more than one-third stay for three years or more, according to the U.S. Department of Labor.

Hourly restaurant wages are unappealing, Schlosser claims, thanks to industry opposition to increases in the hourly minimum wage. He ignores research out of Florida State University and Miami University of Ohio that found nearly two-thirds of minimum wage employees earn a raise within one to 12 months on the job—half of those received an annual raise of 7 percent or more after inflation.

Eager to dissuade young people from embarking on a restaurant career, Mr. Schlosser consistently fails to mention how hourly wages frequently lead to better opportunities. Four out of every five salaried restaurant employees began their careers working for hourly wages. He also likes to claim that restaurant managers earn about $25,000 a year. In fact, U.S. Department of Labor figures show that quick-service restaurant managers earn an average of more than $44,000 annually.

Ignoring the Opportunities

Young people reading Schlosser would never learn that the restaurant industry is the nation's largest private-sector employer and growing faster than the nation's economy. He ignores the professional opportunities the restaurant industry creates as the largest employer of minority managers, and the fact that more hospitality businesses are owned by African-Americans, Hispanics and Asian-Americans than the national average.

Another misleading Schlosser theme is workplace safety. While no workplace is accident-free, he never mentions that the rate of occupational injuries in the restaurant industry is lower than the average for all workplaces and has been falling for years. In fact, restaurants are safer than many other popular teen employment choices, Occupational Safety and Health Administration reports show.

Young readers also can expect to read Schlosser's baseless but often-repeated claim that in 2003 "almost the same numbers of fast-food workers were murdered on the job as police officers." In reality, government statistics show that quick-service restaurant employees not only are safer in this regard than police officers, but also than those individuals working in the very bookstores selling Mr. Schlosser's book.

Of course, no Schlosser attack would be complete without blaming our industry for childhood weight gain and obesity. But again, the hard facts refute him. While childhood obesity has increased over the last 20 years, that has not been matched by increased caloric intake. Former Food and Drug Administration Commissioner Mark McClellan said, "Actual levels of caloric intake among the young haven't appreciably changed in 20 years."

Nutrition experts remind us that weight gain is caused by burning fewer calories than we consume, yet Schlosser ignores unfortunate but critical trends in physical exercise. The number of children biking or walking to school has dropped 70 percent within a generation. And almost one in four children ages 9 to 13 engage in no physical activity at all, according to the Centers for Disease Control and Prevention.

Changed for the Better

Mr. Schlosser claims to write in the tradition of legendary muckraker Upton Sinclair, whose 1906 expose of unsanitary food processing marks its centennial this year [2006]. Sadly, Schlosser's *Chew On This* lacks the objectivity of Sinclair's *The Jungle.*

Instead of distorting reality, Schlosser should have explained how the intervening 100 years transformed our society from one in which an estimated 2 million children went to bed hungry each night to one where America's food is safer, more affordable and more abundant than ever before. Our industry helped make that happen. But why let the facts get in the way of a good story?

Fast Food Nation Highlights the Food Industry's Ability to Thwart Meaningful Regulation

Bill Whit

Bill Whit is a professor of sociology at Grand Valley State University in Michigan.

In the viewpoint that follows, Whit uses Eric Schlosser's Fast Food Nation *and Marion Nestle's* Food Politics: How the Food industry Influences Health and Nutrition *to explain how the food industry is contributing to health and social problems in the United States. After discussing the poor nutritional value of fast food meals and the minimum-wage jobs created in this market, Whit launches into what he sees as the most troublesome aspect of the industry—its influence over government and legislation. Using arguments from Schlosser and Nestle, Whit contends that the food industry has powerful lobbying strength in Congress, keeping regulation of products and wages at a minimum. He even asserts that the industry has enough influence to render existing legislation ineffective.*

"Rationalization for profit," is how the 1986 video *Hamburger 1, McProfit,* summarized trends in our food system. A comparison of expenditures for fast foods indicates the amplitude of change in eating practices over the last generation: In 1970, Americans spent roughly six billion dollars on take-out and other fast foods; by the year 2000, this amount had skyrocketed to a staggering 110 billion dollars. If rationalization is an economic concept and profits fill the pockets of a few large firms, the perverse effects are all too noticeable in

Bill Whit, "Food Politics: How the Food Industry Influences Health and Nutrition/Fast Food Nation: The Dark Side of the All-American Meal." Reproduced by permission of Taylor & Francis Group, LLC, www.taylorandfrancis.com.

the United States where roughly 60 percent of the population is overweight and 30 percent is obese. Heart disease and diabetes are on the rise too. And without pushing the analogy, it is possible to argue that our well- but ill-fed society is on the verge of committing nutricide.

The two books under review here provide a great deal of information on the reorganization of the American food system. Marion Nestle's *Food Politics* is an insider's look at what happened to her as a nutritionist as she interacted with food producers and government regulatory agencies. Eric Schlosser's *Fast Food Nation* evidences muckraking journalism in his exposé of fast food, its suppliers, regulators, and customers.

Problems of the Food Industry

The insights of both of these authors neatly encapsulate the major problems of the fast food industry. For example, gigantism characterizes much of the food production and distribution sector today. Corporate industrialized agriculture crowds small and medium sized farmers out of existence. As noted in *Fast Food Nation*, the development of oligopsony [a skewed market in which a small number of buyers controls a product or service] in food growing is of great concern. Specifically with potatoes, "a few large buyers now dominate the landscape of small growers." Similarly beef production has moved from cows grazing on grass to gigantic feed lots which increase disease and pollute the environment. Schlosser notes that each cow in these food lots produces daily 50 pounds of manure and urine, which is dumped into lagoons and pollutes ground water. In these less-than-healthy fattening paddocks, it has become necessary to overuse antibiotics to prevent endemic cattle sickness. The result is that germs are now more resistant, and many sources document this decreasing efficacy of antibiotics.

Both books note the foisting of unnutritional and junk food on schools, colleges, and universities. As funding for education is reduced, exclusive contracts with fast food producers and soda companies provide the funds for extracurricular activities such as sports and music. They also have encouraged rapid increases in obesity to the point of this problem rivaling smoking as a health hazard. Fast food also affects youth by providing minimalist salaries without fringe benefits.

Other researchers show that McDonald's and its fast food friends target children as "consumers in training." Sponsoring playlands and birthday parties for young people entraps children and their parents. American analysts of family behavior have noted that children, often by their nagging, control the food restaurant selection of adults in middle class America. McDonald's benefits from this dynamic.

Corporate food giants also strive to influence education in the classroom. This includes the providing of educational materials on nutrition. And, as Nestle notes, increasingly corporations fund and control the research about nutrition and eating in state universities. She reports that "[i]n the Department of Plant and Microbial Biology at the University of California, Berkeley" there has developed a "partnership" whereby the industry partner would:

- select the participating faculty;
- have free access to all uncommitted results of participating faculty;
- review research results prior to publication;
- veto faculty participation in other projects; and
- place a full-time scientist of its own on the faculty.

Little wonder then that our best interests are not being served by this academy-corporation nexus. So what should we, as citizens in a democracy, expect from the government?

Corporate Influence in Government

Crucial to the perspectives of both of these important books, is the analysis of the manner in which corporate attempts to influence the political system exhibit hegemony over the interests and health of food consumers. Among the manners in which corporate food interests successfully influence government for their own accumulative purposes are: campaign contributions, lobbying, informal gatherings, revolving door personnel (between government and industry), and lawsuits. Historically important was the 1972 contribution of Ray Crock [*sic*] of McDonald's to the [Richard] Nixon [presidential] campaign of $250,000 to create a subminimum wage that was 20 percent lower. It enabled fast food employers to pay $1.28 per hour to their high school employees.

Industry spends annually $2.7 million lobbying each member of Congress. This goes for such expenses as campaign contributions, partisan information, as well as "socializing at dinner parties, receptions, meetings, golf games, birthday parties and weddings" and paying for vacations and speaking fees [according to Nestle]. This amounted to $1.42 billion of food industry lobbying pressure on Congress. As Nestle writes:

> In the 1950s, just 25 groups of food producers dominated agricultural lobbying. But by the mid 1980s there were 84 such groups. And by the late 1900s, there were hundreds—if not thousands—of business associations, and individuals attempting to influence federal decisions relating to every conceivable aspect of food and beverage production, manufacture, sales, service and trade.

She continues, "the hundreds of millions of dollars available to the meat and dairy lobbies through check-off programs . . . and the billions of dollars that food companies spend on advertising and lawsuits, so far exceed both the amounts spent by the federal government on nutritional advice for the public and the annual budget of any consumer advocacy group that they cannot be considered in the same stratosphere."

As many political commentators have noted, there exists a "revolving door" between personnel in government and personnel in private industry. The new USDA [US Department of Agriculture] secretary, John Block, was an Illinois hog farmer. During his confirmation hearings, he had remarked that he was "not so sure government should get into telling people what they should or should not eat." Further, [Nestle writes,] "two high-level USDA positions had been filled by a former executive director of the American Meat Institute and a lobbyist for the National Cattleman's Association (a tradition cherished to this day)."

Using the Courts to Thwart Opposition

When these means of pressure fail to accomplish corporate goals, these same corporations resort to the legal system. Most famous is the "McLibel" suit in England where McDonald's sued two members of Greenpeace who had passed out information critical of McDonald's food offerings. There, Greenpeace members leafleted McDonald's claiming that, "Meat . . . was responsible for 70% of all food poisoning incidents and antibiotics, hormones and pesticides in annual feed damage the health of 'people on a meat-based diet.'" The resulting trial illustrated the ties and expense to which a food company was willing to go to stifle critics over such practices.

Indeed, Oprah Winfrey, the U.S. talk show host, was sued by the beef industry in 1996 after interviewing a "vegetarian activist" critical of that industry. Although Winfrey won, her legal fees exceeded $1 million. There could be no better way to inhibit further lawsuits.

One would think that the U.S. regulatory agencies—appointed by the executive branch and approved by Congress—would mitigate some of these greater corporate excesses. Specifically, regulatory agencies like the U.S. Department of Agriculture (USDA), the Federal Drug Administration [*sic*] (FDA), and the Occupational Safety and Health Agency [*sic*] (OSHA) could act in the interest of all of us. But the fact is that the same kinds of pressure food corporations bring to bear on legislatures also have hegemonic implications for the way in which regulatory agencies can realize and fulfill their mission. A revolving door policy often puts the "fox in the chicken pen." Options open to inhibit regulation are: underfunding, understaffing, and mollifying the intent of laws designed to protect the public.

Regulations with No Bite

We now find ourselves in a regulatory environment where the U.S. Department of Agriculture cannot even mandate a recall of bad meat. New to our era is feed lot beef, which Schlosser describes: "Far from the natural habitat, the cattle feed lots become more prone to all sorts of illnesses. 'Waste products from poultry plants . . . are also being fed to cattle.' This chicken manure may contain dangerous bacteria such as *salmonella* and *campylobacter* such as tape worm and *giardia lamblia*, antibiotic residue, arsenic and heavy metals." *E. coli* 057:H7 is in one percent of meat and is spread to other meat in grinding up beef for hamburgers. "A single animal infected with *E. coli* 0157:H7 can contaminate 32,000 pounds of that ground beef." Today the USDA often allows a food company that is in violation of government standards for meat to write its own announcement. Often that document can sound more like an advertisement for the company than a meat recall.

Another instance of industrial hegemony involves the Occupational Safety and Health Agency. As Schlosser writes,

> When Ronald Reagan was elected president in 1980, OSHA was already underfunded and understaffed . . . a typical American employer could expect an OSHA inspector about once in every 80 years. Nevertheless, the Reagan administration was determined to reduce OSHA's authority even further as part of a push for deregulation. The number of OSHA inspectors was eventually cut by 20%, and in 1981 their agency adopted a new policy of "voluntary compliance."

Nestle notes the effects of this in the Health Food industry. Since the Dietary Supplement and Health and Education Act of 1994 (DSHEA), "the FDA has not banned a single supplement—not even a few products they believe harmful." The FDA's billion dollar budget of 2001 included only $6 million for dietary supplement regulation. Employees, exhausted by relentless pressure from members of Congress or their staff, leave the agency in droves further depleting its resources.

The Authors' Solutions

What needs to be done? Both authors advocate personal and institutional solutions. Among the personal ones are declaring oneself an "ad free zone," eating only at individually owned restaurants, exercising more, and [supporting] what has become the "Slow Food" movement. In fact Nestle recognizes that many well-educated people have already done these things. Collective solutions to these social problems include getting soda out of the schools (as a Los Angeles district has just done), subsidizing healthy food in vending machines, outlawing television food ads for children and, as with the new dietary guidelines, mandating exercise in school.

Nevertheless, from the perspective of critical sociology, this really is not enough. The problems that have resulted in the greatest obesity in history, come from the massive hegemonic control over legislators, regulatory agencies, schools, and nutrition research that corporations exercise. Both Nestle and Schlosser point us toward the disturbing conclusion that we are living out a societal disengagement between healthy human nutrition and the capitalist imperative to maximize profits which may ultimately lead to a nutricidal food system in the world's richest country.

The Market Will Ultimately Determine Whether *Fast Food Nation*'s Suggestions Are Worth Considering

Gary Alan Fine

The author of Kitchens: The Culture of Restaurant Work, *Gary Alan Fine is also a sociology professor and director of graduate student affairs at Northwestern University in Evanston, Illinois.*

Fine argues in the following viewpoint that Eric Schlosser's Fast Food Nation *is an emotional work that unfortunately does not think through its proposed solutions to the "problem" of fast food and the food industry. According to Fine, after condemning the industry for luring Americans into eating unhealthy food and establishing a business model that attracts only minimum-wage workers, Schlosser suggests that government intervention is needed to right these and other wrongs. Fine, however, contends that this industry thrives because people like and want fast food; it is their choice to patronize these establishments. In addition, Fine maintains that the fast food industry supplies millions of jobs to unskilled workers who otherwise might not be employed. Finally, Fine believes that government regulation is not the solution to any perceived ills in the industry. He insists that consumer pressure is the force that always dictates winners and losers in the marketplace, influencing owners to maintain health standards and attend to other concerns for fear of losing customers.*

There is a tightly held, though empirically misguided, belief that no one ever went broke underestimating the taste of the American public. This claim can be applied equally to

Gary Alan Fine, "Chewing the Fat," *Reason*, vol. 33, no. 6, November, 2001. Reproduced by permission.

mass-market restaurateurs and high-end authors. The latter routinely hector readers about what we should eat, as if we were the most irresponsible, spoiled tots, and they the most sagacious parents. For a clear window into the mind of such a scold, skip Eric Schlosser's title [*Fast Food Nation*] for his subtitle. Schlosser, a correspondent for *The Atlantic*, has dubbed his bestselling account of the fast food industry, "The Dark Side of the All-American Meal." No delicacy here.

Schlosser is not pleased with inexpensive, franchised chain restaurants. In his introduction he asserts, in what must be one of the most charming acts of literary balance, "I do not mean to suggest that fast food is solely responsible for every social problem now haunting the United States." Well, it's good to get that out of the way! As with many entrepreneurs seeking their fortunes by identifying and solving oh-so-pressing social problems, Schlosser's professed concern is with "the nation's children" and the impact of this industry that "feeds off the young."

A Thriving Industry Enjoyed by Patrons

Like pornography, fast food gets no respect. Here is a successful, lively business with many critics and few public champions. To be sure, corporations puff up themselves in their advertisements, but they spout in a vacant echo chamber. Yet we must ask: If everyone hates fast food, how and why does the industry thrive?

Schlosser claims that fast food does so well because of government policies that support and subsidize the industry. At the same time, he argues, there's an absence of controls over fast food's supposed excesses, the result being much damage to our health, environment, work force, and economy. He alleges that changes in our economic structure have led to a concentration of unfettered power in the fast food world, despite the contempt of elite commentators. Schlosser doesn't attack fast food on its aesthetic dimension, on its tackiness and taste. Indeed, he avers that most of it tastes "pretty good," although he inserts the rather odd dig that "it has been carefully designed to taste good." Perhaps not so different from the menus at [haute cuisine restaurants] Lutece or Chez Panisse.

For Schlosser, though, "the real price never appears on the menu." We need to "know what really lurks between those sesame-seed buns." We are warned that fast food has contributed to obesity, the malling of America, the destruction of small farms and rain forests, occupational hazards, the threat of tainted meat, and the destruction of workers' rights. Schlosser concludes that, "The profits of the fast food chains have been made possible by losses imposed on the rest of society." Happy Meals, it would seem, have a lot to answer for.

While I doubt much of Schlosser's political and economic assessment, he is a lively writer, and can make a story come alive with his ability to present heroes and villains. He knows how to write non-fiction, and effectively (if romantically) presents the lives of people affected by the fast food industry.

Heroes and Villains

There is the Horatio Alger–like[1] sharecropper's son, Carl Karcher, the creator of Carl's Jr. restaurants, eventually fired and locked out by his corporate board. There is Dave Feamster, a struggling and solicitous owner of a Little Caesars pizza franchise. There is Hank, the frustrated cattle rancher, whose suicide, we are assured, was at least partially the result of economic changes wrought by the fast food industry. There is Elisa Zamot, the working-class Colorado teen, who rises before dawn only to be underpaid and mistreated by McDonald's. There is Kenny Dobbins, a loyal meat packer severely injured and abused by the packing industry. Schlosser sees the land-

1. Nineteenth-century author Horatio Alger is known for his novels about boys who rise from poverty to wealth.

scapes of culinary America (and now the world) littered by the battered and bruised bodies of workers exploited by those more powerful.

Fast Food Nation is rife with villains as well. Many are large, impersonal corporations, all too often hiding behind vaguely sinister acronyms (IBP, CKE, IFF). Others are the directors of these large, "faceless" organizations, always presented without the sympathetic understanding that Schlosser so effectively grants to their underlings.

Academics sometimes refer to this style of writing as "sociology with adjectives," referring to the power of the pungent, descriptive phrase to set the terms of debate without having to adduce evidence. Consider, for instance, the difference between a "sizzling burger" and a "leaden burger." Such descriptions, sprinkled like salt throughout *Fast Food Nation*, affect the taste of the repast. Schlosser is an adjectival writer, a scribe who deftly deploys literary condiments.

Dirty Jobs, but Jobs Nonetheless

But to dismiss Schlosser's rhetorical flourishes is not to dismiss his arguments. Every industry has its own peculiarities, many of them unpleasant. Recall the famous analogy between sausage-making and lawmaking that suggests watching either process is unappealing. The backstage of most production techniques have this underground quality, and meatpacking and food preparation certainly hold to this unappetizing tradition (as everyone has known from the 1906 muckraking of Upton Sinclair's *The Jungle* onward). Schlosser's descriptions are searing, no doubt. No picnics here; blood and guts are the decorative touches on the work floors. The mass processing of food is inevitably a case of what the sociologist Everett Hughes termed "dirty work"—necessary for a society's survival, but not nice. Hospital operating rooms, battlefields, and sanitation trucks also fall under this category. We turn our faces away, until others force our faces back.

Such dirty workplaces contribute jobs that keep people alive, both by giving them things they need or by providing them with work by which to feed themselves. To be sure, these are jobs that neither Schlosser nor most of his readers would dream of except in their worst nightmares. Yet low-skill natives and far-flung immigrants take these unappealing jobs because they conclude that their lives will be markedly improved by such work. Their choice is not to write for *The Atlantic* [like Schlosser] or for *REASON* [like Fine]. Schlosser accurately points to the dangers of mass meat processing, but danger is endemic to the human condition.

Unnecessary danger can be curtailed, but federal regulators, juries, and journalists may not be able to distinguish necessary from unnecessary. Schlosser has a sensitive nose, but would these workers prefer to find their jobs gone because of the fine sensitivities of canny writers? No one should argue against corporate ethics and morality—they are heavenly virtues. The controversy is over who will—who is capable of—adequately cleaning up the mess when that morality is not in evidence. Schlosser presents no evidence that government inspectors have been effective in such situations; the marked improvement in working conditions since the days of Upton Sinclair is due at least as much to technological advancements that increase efficiency. After all, routinely injuring or killing workers is no way to keep a mobile work force happy.

The Public Keeps the Industry in Line

It's also no way to keep customers satisfied. Despite Schlosser's animus toward fast food, the evidence indicates that the fast food industry contributes to the improvement of sanitary and work conditions. The providers of consumer services to a large public are particularly susceptible to consumer pressure, and especially wary of poisoning their customers. When in 1993 Jack in the Box hamburgers caused *E. coli* illnesses and four deaths, the corporation took steps to protect their meat

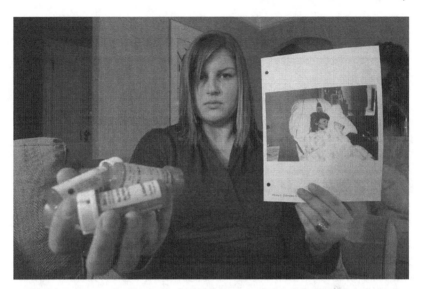

In this 2008 photograph, Alyssa Chrobuck, who was a victim of the 1993 Jack in the Box restaurant E. coli outbreak, displays a photograph of herself as a child in her hospital bed, along with some of the many medications she takes, fifteen years later, for lasting health problems her doctors have attributed to her contamination with E. coli. © AP Images/ Elaine Thompson.

supply. Whether from moral concern or a desire to avoid bad publicity and lawsuits, one big, faceless corporation succeeded in changing the way that meat was processed, at least for its customers. Evil meatpackers were at the mercy of their supposed corporate comrades-in-arms, the fast food industry.

In a similar way, public pressure on fast food corporations to eliminate plastic packaging, the destruction of the rain forest, or the reduction of fatty oils has proven to be effective. A food industry without large, influential corporations that consumers can rally against would be far less amenable to change. It is precisely the public presence of ubiquitous fast food chains that permits social movements to challenge the industry effectively. A small change in market share may be the difference between profit and bankruptcy for those corporations.

All of the so-called problems of the fast food industry could be solved by similar public pressure, if those issues were truly important to the public. Public pressure could increase pay scales for young workers like Elisa Zamot, if the same public would be willing to patronize those corporations that provided workers with a "living wage." Students at Harvard, in their successful sit-in on behalf of their cleaning crews, showed the way. Harvard's tuition is inelastic—what is a few thousand dollars among friends compared to $11 an hour? Perhaps the same might be true at Taco Bell; perhaps not.

Government Intervention

Like so many activists, Schlosser's arguments operate on several tracks. The public should rise up in righteous indignation against fast food—both through public pressure on the restaurant chains and through pressuring the government to enact ever more regulations to make the pain vanish. But whether government regulation will be as effective in changing corporate practices as that of consumer pressure is an issue that Schlosser doesn't consider.

One virtue of Schlosser's analysis is to remind us of the extent of governmental intervention in the market, and not only on the side of the workers. The fast food chains receive hundreds of millions of dollars in government subsidies for training workers through the Work Opportunity Tax Credit program. Schlosser points out that we are subsidizing the fast food industry for training workers, even if these workers quit or are fired after working for less than six months.

Even if we accept the questionable assertion that government should provide tax incentives for hiring untrained workers—most of whom would be hired in the natural course of doing business—are these the long-term jobs that taxpayers should support? Assuredly not. Similarly, state government use of subsidies to attract corporate headquarters may work in the short-term: The state of Nebraska used such techniques to lure Iowa Beef Packers to Dakota City, Nebraska, an effective strategy until South Dakota offered a still-better deal. These government baubles lead to a climate in which the next, more attractive subsidy will have a louder siren call.

Fast Food Is a Personal Choice

When all the talk of the injustice and crimes has become half-forgotten echoes in most eaters' heads, there is still the food to deal with. What tobacco was to the 1990s, fat may become to the current decade. Increasingly we hear cries for a "fat tax." Fast food can be blamed, claims one waggish commentator, for the creation of "Gen-XL." Fast food, of course, includes a wide range of foods, including salads, but the mainstays— hamburgers, fried chicken, and tacos—have been criticized for high fat and sodium content. Schlosser claims that the "annual cost of obesity is now twice as large as the fast food industry's total revenues"—a factoid justified by one journalist quoting another. Supposedly 44 million Americans are obese, and another 6 million are super-obese.

Given the (ever-growing) government involvement in health care, the medical costs of fat have become a public policy issue of grave import. We are told that the government must curtail our freedom to choose our own food in order to cut its costs—costs that it assumed through the expansion of government into health care in the first place. Each government intervention legitimates further intervention, until the entire camel, not just its nose, is under the tent.

I do not claim that fast food is a culinary masterpiece, but the proof of the pudding is in the eating. De gustibus non [est] disputandum [i.e., taste is not something to be disputed]. As a former restaurant reviewer, I do not patronize fast food establishments often, but as Schlosser admits, the food is created to taste good—and taste good it often does. Fast food is, certainly, a choice, and one's food choices ought to be personal matters. There seems to be no market as open and as accessible with as many options as the restaurant industry, with thousands of choices in any mid-sized city.

The explosive growth of fast food restaurants over the course of the past several decades should tell us something: Fast food does not always satisfy one's highest aspirations— much less the refined sensibilities of journalists. But it certainly fills one's tummy passably well.

Fast Food Nation Focuses Too Much on Criticizing the Corporatization of Food

Steven A. Shaw

Steven A. Shaw practiced law before founding the website eGullet, which focuses on culinary topics. He also wrote the book Turning the Tables: Restaurants from the Inside Out.

Many reviewers of Eric Schlosser's book Fast Food Nation *have lauded its portrayal of the fast food industry and the myriad problems of corporate control exerted by companies that dominate it. Schlosser argues in the book that, among other evils resulting from this control, food suppliers have succumbed to corporatization in an attempt to fulfill these restaurants' demands and that fast food companies have implemented worker and wage policies that demean their workers. In the viewpoint that follows, Shaw contends that this portrayal of fast food corporations results from Schlosser's intense dislike of the capitalist system, which leads to a narrow and unenlightening industry critique that fails to address the problems that do exist. Shaw insists that had Schlosser been able to widen his view beyond the obvious vilification of corporate fast food, he would have been able to better probe the causes of fast food's control over the American diet, food supply chain, and worker policy.*

The airwaves, editorial pages, and Internet chat groups—not to mention the "Dining In, Dining Out" section of the *New York Times*—are awash in indignation over the revelations contained in *Fast Food Nation*. In a series of meticulous and riveting exposés—ranging from "Why the Fries Taste

Steven A. Shaw, "Happy Meal?," *Commentary*, May 2001. Reprinted from COMMENTARY, May 2001, by permission; copyright © 2001 by Commentary, Inc.

Good" (artificial flavoring) to "The Most Dangerous Job" (meatpacking)—Eric Schlosser, a correspondent for the *Atlantic*, builds a compelling case against the fast-food industry based on the premise that "the real price never appears on the menu." Then he tells us exactly what he thinks that price is.

The Evils of the Fast Food Nation

The fast-food business, Schlosser's story goes, started innocently enough in the aftermath of World War II as the innovation of a few iconoclasts like Ray Kroc of McDonald's and Carl Karcher of the Carl's Jr. chain, both of whom sought to feed southern California's expanding population in a manner suited to the new automobile culture, and to make a buck in the process. At this stage, Schlosser's admiration for his subjects is evident. But as the fast-food phenomenon spread across the land, driven in large part by the construction of the interstate highway system, things went terribly wrong. Rugged individualism gave way to conformity, and entrepreneurship gave way to corporate hegemony.

Today, argues Schlosser, the fast-food industry is responsible for, or at least symptomatic of, a host of societal ills. Driven by greed, McDonald's and its ilk have created a labor economy dependent on cheap, unskilled, part-time employees, mostly teenagers who cannot easily protect their interests by unionizing. They have also fundamentally transformed the whole spectrum of the American agricultural system, from potato farming to meatpacking, making it into a reflection of their own corporate operations and encouraging the exploitation of family farmers, ranchers, immigrant laborers, and the soil.

Worse, wielding the dual weapons of advertising and political lobbying, the fast-food industry seeks to control our economy, our government, and our very psyches, particularly those of our children. By targeting the young and impressionable—including through insidious advertising in the public schools—these multinational corporations create captive consumers who can he relied upon to pester their parents for unhealthy food and the toy trinkets used to promote it. All the while, companies reveal themselves as the worst kind of hypocrites, trumpeting the free market while covertly lobbying for subsidies and preferential regulatory treatment.

Nor does the litany of evils end there. The industry is, it seems, largely responsible for obesity, for dangerous levels of contaminants in our meat supply, for failing to maintain workplace safety, and for high rates of suicide among cattle ranchers. Through the carefully plotted use of additives, the industry's flavor engineers—flavorists, as they are called—dupe us into enjoying what is essentially flavorless frozen-and-reheated food. And as fast food spreads beyond these shores and throughout the industrialized world, other nations arc rapidly falling prey to the same ills.

The Capitalist System Run Amok

It should come as no surprise to learn that Schlosser profoundly distrusts the capitalist system: this, if anything, is the underlying theme of *Fast Food Nation*. Although he concedes that "the market is a tool, and a useful one," no good, it seems, has ever been achieved by the market except insofar as its impulses have been strictly circumscribed by hard-hitting regulatory schemes.

In this respect, the fast-food companies represent, for Schlosser, the capitalist system run amok, rendering moot the conventional wisdom of supply and demand and making brainwashed addicts of us all. Indeed, Schlosser writes, just as the 20th century was "dominated by the struggle against totalitarian systems of state power," so the present century will be marked by "a struggle to curtail excessive corporate power." He appears to intend the analogy quite exactly: in a chapter on the relationship between Ray Kroc and Walt Disney, there are hints of shared Nazi tendencies.

Responding to customers' need for speed, McDonald's makes fast food even faster by adding second drive-through lanes to some of its restaurants, including this one in Rosemont, Illinois, photographed in 2006. © Tim Boyle/Getty Images.

Unfortunately, to credit this portrait of the fast-food industry as a new evil empire, agribusiness as the reincarnation of Soviet collectivized farming, and capitalism as the new Communism, one must not only discount Schlosser's wild hyperbole but overlook the inconvenient fact that capitalism has been responsible for almost every instance of material good since the industrial revolution. Even Schlosser is compelled to admit that the industry provides gainful employment to many of society's most disadvantaged members, and helps them learn good basic work habits, complaining all the while that its motives in doing so are "hardly altruistic." About that much, at least, he is right: it is on account of profit, not warm feelings, that America's 3.5 million fast-food workers get paid.

The Public Wants Fast Food

It is a pity Schlosser's mind is so relentlessly preoccupied by politics, and a callow politics at that. For as someone who wants to reduce the nation's consumption of fast food, he fully understands that his many top-down proposals in this direction—a ban on advertising directed at children, a new federal food-safety agency, lots more government regulations, and so forth—will only take him so for. If consumers are to alter their behavior, they will have to be offered something better—and they will have to want it.

Schlosser is dimly aware of this conundrum. "Nobody in the United States is forced to buy fast food," he writes in a rare moment of illumination, adding, "The first step toward meaningful change is by far the easiest: stop buying it." But there is the crux of the matter. If customers wanted better-tasting or more nutritious fast food, surely the money-mad corporations would be providing it. But every attempt to create such items (like the McLean Deluxe, made partly from seaweed derivatives) has been an abject failure. Nobody wants to eat them.

A Failure of Taste

In short, fast food does not explain our culture; our culture explains fast food. In his pursuit of corporate perfidy, Schlosser never pauses to consider that the industry itself is just one of the reasons for the fast-fooding of America, which owes its existence to factors ranging from the decline of the family (the enjoyment of good food must be taught by example, beginning in the home), to the entrenchment of career-oriented feminism (it seems almost slanderous today to speak of recipes being handed down from mother to daughter), to the wholesale rejection of the idea of a distinctive American culture, including the (admittedly slender) culinary one.

Of all the arguments against fast food, the strongest and most obvious is the one Schlosser does not and seemingly cannot make: that its popularity represents a failure not of market capitalism but of taste. In fact, he summarily dismisses any such thesis as the carping of elitists. "The aesthetics of fast food," he writes in the book's introduction, "are of much less concern to me than its impact upon the lives of ordinary

Americans, both as workers and consumers." And besides, he adds, his populist instincts momentarily getting the better of his anti-capitalist ones, fast food tastes "pretty good."

Well, taken in moderation, fast food is undoubtedly harmless, and only marginally less healthful than the food served at the family-run diners of old. It can also satisfy particular cravings for fat, sugar, and salt. But as compared with what does it taste "pretty good"? This is a question Schlosser is unequipped to answer, and perhaps even to ask, though it would lead to a much more nuanced and interesting discussion of the pros and cons of a fast-food nation. And in the meantime, in the person of the big, evil, multinational corporation, a more convenient target lies at hand.

The *Fast Food Nation* Movie Fails to Communicate the Book's Messages

Dave Hoskin

Dave Hoskin is a journalist and film critic in Australia.

After deciding to adapt his book to film, Eric Schlosser decided to forgo the obvious medium for the movie—documentary—in favor of a fictional adaptation he developed with director Richard Linklater, known for such movies as Dazed and Confused *and* Waking Life. *Schlosser worried that a documentary version of the book would fail in its attempt to present the material with force; however, Hoskin argues in the following viewpoint, that the fictionalized movie version of the book falls short of portraying the book's main arguments in a compelling manner. Hoskin believes that the book aptly presents a wide range of problems resulting from the fast food industry's prominent position in American society, and he laments the movie's inability to do the same. This problem, he maintains, stems from a fictionalization of issues instead of stories, and is made worse by a focus on minutiae, lack of character development, and all around poor creative choices. All these shortcomings result in a film that Hoskin characterizes as contrived and patronizing of its audience.*

The most memorable moment in [the 2006 movie adaptation of] *Fast Food Nation* sees Greg Kinnear look across a restaurant table at Bruce Willis and say, 'There's shit in the meat.' Willis glares back at Kinnear, and after ranting about whiners ruining America with their complaints about food contamination, he takes a bite from his hamburger. 'It's a sad fact of life, but the truth is we've all got to eat a little shit from time to time,' he mutters. The scene's obviously intended to be about America's contaminated meat supply, but it's tempting to see it as a metaphor. *Fast Food Nation* is an adaptation of Eric Schlosser's book of the same name, and like the film its principle concerns are purity and consumption. However in translating those concerns to the screen, certain creative decisions have been made, decisions that have ironically compromised the purity of Schlosser's work. The result is that while the book is an intelligent, well-argued piece of journalism, Linklater's film takes the same basic material and manages to make it unpalatable.

Put simply, somehow shit has got into the meat.

Fictionalized Issues, Not Events

To be fair, *Fast Food Nation* was never going to be the easiest book to bring to the screen. Where similar films like [Morgan Spurlock's 2004 critique of the unhealthy effects of subsisting on fast food] *Super Size Me* or [the 1998 film by directors Franny Armstrong and Ken Loach detailing the English lawsuit brought by two environmentalists against McDonald's] *McLibel* have obvious protagonists to hang their narrative upon, Schlosser's book is trickier because of its determinedly holistic approach. Although singling out McDonald's for criticism, Schlosser's gaze encompasses the industry as a whole and the culture it has fostered. There is no obvious narrative, a preponderance of statistical and scientific data, and no protagonist unless we count Schlosser's authorial voice. Furthermore the emotional temperature of this voice remains cool throughout, and although the book has been heavily attacked, Schlosser notes in the afterword of the 2002 [paperback] edition that, 'thus far the critics have failed to cite any errors in the text'.

The logical form for packaging such a book for cinematic consumption would therefore be documentary. Anti-corporate documentaries have a good track record both critically and financially, with some of the most notable, such as [the 2005 documentary directed by Alex Gibney about the Enron Corporation scandal] *Enron: The Smartest Guy in the Room* based on pre-existing material. However, Schlosser claims that he never completely trusted the people who proposed this kind of adaptation, and worried they would soft pedal the material. The interesting thing is that because of this understandable desire for editorial purity, Schlosser and Linklater decided to fictionalize the material. On the face of it, this isn't really a revolutionary idea as plenty of films blur the boundaries between fiction and journalism. For instance, the makers of *The Insider* [a 1999 movie directed by Michael Mann about a tobacco industry whistleblower] and *All the President's Men* [the 1976 film by director Alan Pakula about the Watergate scandal] are quite open about the fact that thriller devices have been inserted into their narratives to heighten the drama. But the essential difference between *Fast Food Nation* and its spiritual forerunners is its commitment to dramatizing issues rather than specific historical events. Thus, whereas the protagonists of *Insider* and *President's Men* are based on real people, *Fast Food Nation* invents characters to represent arguments from Schlosser's book. Some of them are more real than others—for instance Kris Kristofferson's old rancher is clearly based on Hank, one of the many interview subjects in Schlosser's book. In general however, the majority of the characters and what passes for a 'storyline' have been invented to provide an overview of an entire industry. Put simply, this is *Traffic* [director Steven Soderbergh's 1999 movie about drug trafficking in the United States] with hamburgers instead of heroin.

Presenting Messages Differently

It's undeniably a lateral approach to adapting tricky material, and in avoiding the more obvious strategies Schlosser and Linklater are to be commended. However, the thing that brings the film undone is the fact that audiences consume stories in different ways, and that consumption depends upon how the story is told. For instance, while documentaries obviously have a point of view, we still tend to watch them expecting to be presented with a series of facts.

Thus when they give us nothing but bad news on a certain subject, as long as those facts are not in dispute (or the dispute is at least acknowledged) we don't tend to feel that we're being hectored. This is bolstered by the fact that the typical tone of a documentary is measured, even muted. They may incorporate spectacular footage or reveal gobsmacking [astonishing] truths, but there's usually a sense that there's some distance between the action and the audience.

Fiction is another kettle of fish altogether, even fiction that purports to be 'based on a true story'. We expect more subtlety, more sophisticated forms of argument, and when we don't get them we feel manipulated. In short, although both modes of storytelling are perfectly valid, fiction plays to different expectations. The subject that it dramatizes may be perfectly true, but if it cannot be engaging and even, dare one say it, entertaining, then it becomes the cinematic equivalent of spinach. Linklater and Schlosser insist that they were trying to avoid this kind of blunt message-film, but somewhere along the line they have gone off the rails spectacularly.

Satire Softens the Message

The first worrying sign is the fact that the filmmakers have elected not to name corporate names. Rather than McDonald's, we're presented with a fictional company called Mickey's, and any illusions that this is a film with teeth are swiftly stifled. Frankly, parodies of McDonald's are pretty passé, and rather than be the filmmaker who distinguishes himself by stabbing his target in the chest, Linklater opts for clunking satire. There's an argument to be made that Mickey's represents the industry as a whole, but that's little more than an excuse for gutlessness. What's the point of constructing this fictional strawman in order to knock it down? Schlosser hasn't pulled his punches in print and yet he still managed to spread more than enough blame around. Certainly McDonald's themselves have not been thrown off by Linklater's cunning ruse, and have done everything they can to debunk *Fast Food Nation* before it even reaches the cinema. Their points are vaguely constructed, selectively argued and do little to advance their cause, but at least they're open about who they're attacking.

The Movie Focuses on Minutiae

More serious is *Fast Fodd Nation*'s failure to integrate its message into a remotely credible piece of cinema. It's obvious that Schlosser and Linklater have tried to cram in as many issues as they can, but they haven't managed to make them dramatic or funny or even very interesting. Even worse, none of the issues they raise feels like they've been examined with any intellectual rigour. One might attribute this to the filmmakers biting off more than they can chew, but films like *Syriana* [director Stephen Gaghan's 2005 film about the politics surrounding the oil industry] or *Lone Star* [the 1996 movie directed by John Sayles about a series of murders discovered after a sheriff is killed] demonstrate that it's possible to encompass broad issues without being facile. The difference is that those films were telling a story and *Fast Food Nation* is not. It shows no interest in weaving its multiple storylines into a greater whole and simply presents us with an intellectually bovine catalogue of horrors that can supposedly be laid at the door of the fast food industry. Rather than take the sensible option of dramatizing Schlosser's most damning charges (for my money the horrific standards of health and safety within the meat-packing industry), or even concentrating on those issues for which the fast food chains cannot fudge responsibility (such as their lousy treatment of their staff), Linklater launches a petty, scattershot assault on every last peccadillo.

For instance, Schlosser's book notes in passing that fast food restaurants have a particularly high likelihood of being robbed, and more often than not the staff commits these robberies. Now this is a nifty little detail but not even remotely close to the core of Schlosser's critique. Linklater, however, cannot resist. In a film already struggling to cram in all the big complex issues he wastes precious time on this. To add insult to injury, he doesn't even have the wit to *simply* show us a crime being committed by the restaurant's employees; instead they stand around and *talk* about it. I mean, *for f---'s sake.*

A Shallow, Crude Interpretation

Now if this kind of cinematic sin were a one-off incident I wouldn't even bring it up. After all, Linklater's films are often shambling gabfests and somehow they manage to work quite well. But at almost every turn *Fast Food Nation* completely and utterly fails to engage the audience. Characters constantly waffle on about what's wrong with various corners of the industry, but it's rare that we see what this means for anyone on the frontlines. The cast is just too big and the issues too diverse, and so they all seem equally shallow. None of the characters ever convince us that they have any interior lives beyond their annoyance with the fast food industry, and so we never really care about them. Once something terrible has happened to them (or more likely once they've *talked* about something terrible happening to them), they're simply forgotten, their function complete.

The trickle-down effect of these lazy creative choices is that rather than being a disturbing piece of activist cinema, *Fast Food Nation* is hilariously crude.

The key to making successful films of this type is a commitment to moral and ethical complexity. For instance, Michael Mann's realization of the whistleblower Jeffrey Wigand was replete with contradictions and rough edges. Wigand might represent the romantic ideal of the little guy up against a corporate behemoth, but he was also overweight, awkward and psychologically spiky. His supposed saviours at *60 Minutes* are little better. They fight hard for Wigand, but they're also deliberately exposing him to potentially dire consequences so that they can exploit his story. *The Insider* might end with its protagonist's vindication, but it's also clear that Big Media can just as easily ruin the little guy as Big Tobacco.

In comparison to this, *Fast Food Nation*'s arguments and revelations seem positively jejune [emaciated]. There are some perfunctory gestures towards presenting an alternative to the film's point of view, but the characters that voice this alternative are no better delineated than their opponents. In fact the most telling moment of all comes when Linklater depicts a group of earnest young things planning to Stick It to The Man by freeing some cows. It's not so much that they're long on idealism and short on practicality—that's what teenagers are *like* after all. No, the problem is that their faux-cynicism, and mouthing of inanities like 'bad guys do bad things until somebody stops them' precisely matches the voice of *Fast Food Nation* as a whole. Linklater might attempt to disguise this by having other characters mock their impotence and naiveté, but it isn't remotely convincing. After all, as previously mentioned, this is a film in which one of the Bad Guys in the System earnestly defends the fact that there is shit in the meat, not because there is some practical obstacle to removing it, but because . . . well, because he's Bad. Where Schlosser's book treats the reader with respect, Linklater's film does not, and this lack of trust in the audience cannot help but be returned in kind.

Artlessness and Cynicism

The most ironic thing about *Fast Food Nation* is that for such a supposedly rebellious film it is disconcertingly intent on being consumed with as little critical thought as possible. Instead it's careful to pick the easiest battles and then fight them in the laziest way possible. Make fun of a big, slow-moving corporate target, snigger at the stupidity of people who think that shit in the meat is acceptable, and dream of one day freeing a cow of your very own. It serves its audience intellectual dross because at a fundamental level it does not trust them, and it's too busy playing at being 'guerrilla cinema' to bother with quaint 'Hollywood' notions like 'character' or 'story'. The stars might feel better for having done something 'political' and the audience might feel smart for having seen something 'political', but this is mere flattery rather than a genuine challenge. Vapid, artless, and cynical in all the worst ways, this is the kind of film that does for dissent what McDonald's does for food.

Unfortunately it also tastes a lot more like shit.

The Documentary
Food, Inc. Expands on
Ideas in *Fast Food Nation*

Robert Kenner, as told to Rebecca Amato and Rahul Hamid

Robert Kenner is a documentary filmmaker who has been a part of numerous PBS documentaries as a director, writer, and producer. At the time this interview was conducted, Rebecca Amato taught social history at New York University and Rahul Hamid was an editor for Cineaste *magazine.*

In June 2009, the documentary Food, Inc. *was released in theaters across the United States. Director Robert Kenner sought to create a film that shows the public the process of food production in America and encourages them to think about how these different systems and methods impact their health and well-being. The following selection presents an interview with Kenner by* Cineaste *magazine in which he discusses the source material for the film—*Fast Food Nation *by Eric Schlosser and* The Omnivore's Dilemma: A Natural History of Four Meals *and* In Defense of Food: An Eater's Manifesto, *both by Michael Pollan—as well as the importance of presenting a wide variety of voices without any overt judgment of these individuals' or corporations' positions. Kenner maintains that by using Schlosser's book as a starting point, he was able to highlight essential issues but enlarge his focus beyond fast food to the food industry as a whole. Further, he emphasizes his desire to make a film that appeals to everyone and accepts the fact that different food choices are necessary for different individuals based on their personal circumstances.*

Rebecca Amato and Rahul Hamid, "The Business of Dinner: An Interview with Robert Kenner," *Cineaste*, vol. 34, no. 3, Summer 2009, pp. 38–41. Copyright © 2009 by Cineaste Publishers, Inc. All rights reserved. Reproduced by permission.

Robert Kenner's new documentary, *Food, Inc.*, could not appear at a more opportune time. [First Lady] Michelle Obama is planting an organic vegetable garden on the White House grounds and articles about sustainable, local, and pesticide-free food seem to appear every week in newspapers and magazines, not just in the lifestyle pages, but in business sections as well. Westchester, New York–raised Kenner has directed and produced several documentaries for public television. . . . Kenner's films have a progressive point of view, but remain committed to a sympathetic and even-handed airing of all sides of an issue. His tone is educational and persuasive. This is particularly welcome when it comes to the popular discourse surrounding food politics, which veers from extreme denial on the part of big industrial food producers to an equally shrill, self-righteous elitism on the part of some food activists.

Many and Varied Voices

Food, Inc. is largely based on [author and journalist] Michael Pollan's two books, *An Omnivore's Dilemma: A Natural History of Four Meals* and *In Defense of Food: An Eater's Manifesto* and Eric Schlosser's *Fast Food Nation*. Both authors appear prominently in the film, providing it with its core values. Kenner adds to their voices from numerous other sources. A former industrial chicken farmer, Carol Morrison, reveals an industrial feedlot, where an endless sea of crowded chickens mill about waiting for slaughter, Morrison loses her contract, because she refuses to change her open-windowed chicken houses to the closed, windowless design required by the company. Kenner's camera pans over acres and acres of industrial cattle feedlots and hog farms. He chronicles the stories of soybean farmers who can no longer save their own seed or plant the varieties they choose due to [chemical giant] Monsanto's near monopoly on pesticide and the genetically modified seeds that are resistant to it. Life-long Republicans Barbara (Barb)

Kowalcyk and her daughter, Patricia Buck, lobby Congress for the passage of Kevin's Law, a bill named in honor of Barbara's son, who died of *E. Coli* poisoning at the age of two. As an antidote, we meet the philosophical Joel Salatin, who raises hogs and cattle on an idyllic farm, and waxes poetic about the glories of the land and of treating animals and produce with the respect they deserve.

Though some of these stories are familiar from other films and books, they are compelling and deserve to be told. Where *Food, Inc.*, excels, however, is in its method of framing these complex elements from the point of view of an educated, socially active consumer—presumably its intended audience. Rather than taking a purely didactic position, forcing us to bear witness to the apparent ugliness of the food industry, Kenner urges viewers to become participants in the democratic system and take responsibility for the food supply. In discussing farm subsidies for the overproduction of corn, Kenner explains how corn products appear not just as sweetener, but also in a huge variety of food additives that are a part of a mind-numbing array of processed foods. The film connects this to the idea that these subsidies and overproduction make it substantially cheaper to eat processed and fast foods, leading not simply to diabetes and obesity among the poor, but also making a switch to a healthier diet a financial impossibility. The film briefly profiles an immigrant family facing just these dilemmas.

Taking this question seriously, Kenner looks not only to sustainable farmers and slow food advocates for answers. He introduces Gary Hirshberg, the head of Stonyfield Farm—one of the largest organic yogurt producers—just as Stonyfield is signing a deal to be sold at Wal-Mart. Hirshberg is eloquent about the power of large-scale production, arguing that this deal will introduce healthy products into more homes, particularly lower income homes, than a thousand farmer's markets. He frankly admits that many of the people with whom he began in the organic movement would see him as a sellout now. The film does not come down on either side of the issue, maintaining a dialectical approach to its subject. In the opening credits, *Food, Inc.* takes on the flashy advertising of food, using a candy-colored supermarket aisle as the setting, with products on the shelves announcing the film's title and makers, suggesting a disconnect between the label and the contents of the package. Not satisfied to once again restate the problems surrounding America's food supply or to disgust the audience with terrible images of industrial slaughter, Kenner ends the film on an optimistic note. With [singer] Bruce Springsteen's soulful cover of "This Land is Your Land" playing in the background, a list of Web sites and organizations dedicated to changing food policy and production standards appear on the screen. *Cineaste* spoke with Kenner in March [2009] about *Food, Inc.* . . .

The Focus Expands Beyond Fast Food

Cineaste: You have said that you and Eric Schlosser had wanted to make a film out of Fast Food Nation *for a long while. During that time Schlosser wrote and produced a fiction film based on the book with Richard Linklater. Did this change your original ideas for the documentary?*

Robert Kenner: Eric did *Fast Food Nation* with Linklater and, as I was developing this and talking about it with people, they felt like they'd already seen *Fast Food Nation* "the documentary" because of Morgan Spurlock's film [*Supersize Me*]. People asked, "Wasn't that already made?" We began to think, wait a second, this is crazy. We've got to hit new ground. Ironically, we were just being funded as this was striking me over the head. So I understood that our original approach had to go—even though I think that Eric's book was about much more than fast food. I realized that we have to make this about how *all* food has become industrialized and to integrate a lot of Michael Pollan's book into this equation. In the midst of synthesizing both Eric and Michael's books, hopefully we could come out with our own point of view as well. So it was a process of discovery, and a scary one, because I didn't know where we were going when we started out.

How did you see your role in terms of making the film? Were you aiming at people who had read the books and sort of figuring out a way to visually describe them and punch home their most significant points, or were you just trying to reach a wider audience in general that may or may not have read the books?

All three of the books, two of Michael's and one of Eric's, were #1 bestsellers. But I had no interest in making a film to convert them; it's not what I wanted to do. I really wanted to find our own voice, and, as a filmmaker, I wanted to figure out how to make it a filmic event. That was very tricky because, on one hand, there's so much freakin' information to deal with, and I wanted to do it without a narrator, and I wanted to try to tell these *vérité* [naturalistic but stylized] stories of the characters, but I wanted them to fit into a much bigger picture.

I wanted to figure out how to do it in an entertaining way. That's where we came up with some of the animation and the style of music and hopefully to inject some touches of humor into a very hard subject. . . .

A Fair View of All Companies

I want to ask you about some of the darker things in the film. The food conglomerates kept you out for the most part, but you still were able to get really compelling footage. How did you connect with some of the people from [chicken producers] Tyson and Perdue who did talk to you?

We pursued Tyson for quite a while and told them about everybody else we were filming. They talked to us but ultimately they were not interested in being filmed or representing their point of view. They did lead us to the National Chicken Council. I felt that if somebody was going to talk to

In March 2012, at a Beef Products Inc. plant, Texas governor Rick Perry demonstrates confidence in "pink slime," a beef product treated with ammonia and used as filler for hamburgers, a truth that was exposed by the 2008 documentary Food, Inc. © AP Images/Nati Harnik.

us we were going to lean over backwards to represent their point of view. With the man from the Chicken Council we put the line in about, "We grow more chickens on less land for fewer dollars." What's wrong with that? I wanted to include his point of view. I think there are things wrong with it, but I also think that it will convince a lot of people. So whenever someone agreed to talk to us we really went out of our way to be fair to them.

But it was amazing how most of the companies did not want to talk to us. They would spend a lot of time asking what we were filming. Monsanto was very curious to know everyone we were talking to, but ultimately did not want to appear. It took a year and a half to get Wal-Mart on camera. They would have been a very easy company to make fun of—

and we didn't give them a free ride—but ultimately they can only benefit from being in the film. So it's not like we're attacking every corporation.

No, actually I thought it was a smart move on Wal-Mart's part.

I did too. If it weren't for Gary Hirshberg, I don't know if they would have shown up, even though we had major connections in their sustainability area who were lobbying for them to film with us. In the area where they are doing good things, I thought, why not try to encourage that? Obviously we're not going into the other issues about Wal-Mart in this movie. We'll leave that for other people.

Local, Sustainable, and Big Organic

I think one of the most interesting contrasts in the film is the one you make between small, local, sustainable production and big organic. What you show on the small farms is obviously very idyllic, but I think Gary Hirshberg makes a very compelling case for the sheer numbers that you can affect with products like Stonyfield Yogurt and Horizon [organic milk products] and even places like [fast Mexican food chain] Chipotle, which was run by McDonald's. The film is pretty even-handed about that question but where do you come down on that issue?

I didn't want to do a "puff piece" about any one of the characters. I made a point of keeping in the film the patron of [holistic, organic farmers] Joel Salatin who said, "We've driven 400 miles to come get this chicken, but it's worth it." Some of my backers kept saying, "Why are you keeping that in?" It's because I didn't want to make Joel just a god, though it sure is attractive and I'd much rather eat his food than anyone else's. Gary was great because he was totally open and I really was appreciative. At the same time there are things that Gary does that I might question. I certainly think local is as important as organic. Gary is very much into organic and he will potentially have to outsource his materials from all over the world.

He runs a large company and that's part of it. When we showed clips at [the event] Slow Food Nation, everyone was very critical of Gary. But I'm not a purist. I think Gary as well as Joel have places to play in this movement. I think there are many spokes to changing this world. I'd rather be able to eat off of Joel's farm, but it's not always practical.

All People Are Called to Arms

Thinking of the Mexican family in the film that eats almost solely fast food because of their income and their lack of time, what answers right now are there for people like them? That leads to the larger issue of how eating sustainably, eating locally and organically, is related to class. How does one separate this from being something that the affluent middle classes do almost as an esthetic gesture?

Well, I think that's the key. We didn't want to make an elitist film. These foods are being priced unfairly, and that's not a coincidence. They're priced comparatively high because we're subsidizing corn. It's not a coincidence that the Mexican family is buying fast food, which is engineered to appeal to people's tastes for sugar, salt, and fat. They're spending billions of dollars to market to these people. And it's artificially cheap. If we were to have a level playing field and we had food stamps that went towards farmer's markets, we could ship a lot of this food at a competitive price. Today the perception is that it's elitist to have good food. But we've made it that way. It's now our job—and hopefully this film's job—to change the way we get our food and to change the artificially low price of this bad food.

I don't know if bad food is the right word . . . or even fast food. It goes beyond fast food. It's the middle road. It's all those unidentifiable words for ingredients in food products. They're all corn and soy products that are being artificially subsidized.

I thought that was one of the strongest parts of the film. We were also really struck by the film's ending and its "call to arms." I was wondering about your decision to do that.

Well, it's a heavy subject that we're dealing with but, at the same time, both Eric and Michael are very optimistic. Our characters—including Gary Hirshberg—are also very optimistic. As much as anything, this is a film about freedom of speech. It really starts to transcend food. I wanted to say that we, as consumers, can make a difference, that we get to vote three times a day. It also goes beyond our actions as consumers because we also want the right to know what's in our food. We have to influence government. It's a difficult situation, but, because we all eat, people are really curious about this subject. They care about what goes into their stomachs. We can change these companies. I just wanted to empower people on some level to believe that we can make a difference. I thought the Bruce Springsteen song was really helpful. It's such a powerful anthem. It's actually a Woody Guthrie song, but Springsteen's rendition is different than any other. . . .

The film is really one that can play to a larger audience because you avoided the "gross-out" scenes that other documentaries about the food supply have used.

Well, we all know there are disgusting things. Listen, the fact is, as Joel says, we're totally removed from where our food comes from. The only slaughter scene we see in the film is on this idyllic farm. I made a point of trying to remove any "gross-out" scenes. I felt like that they weren't going to teach us anything new and would only keep people away.

Social Issues in Literature

CHAPTER 3

Contemporary Perspectives on the Food Industry

The Global Food Movement Has Improved Food Production Worldwide

Frances Moore Lappé

American writer and activist Frances Moore Lappé wrote the influential book Diet for a Small Planet *in 1971. She is the founder of the Institute for Food and Development Policy (aka Food First) and the Center for Living Democracy and continues to write and speak extensively on hunger, poverty, and environmental and societal issues.*

In her book Diet for a Small Planet, *Lappé argues that world hunger resulted from poor food policy, particularly meat production centered on grain feeding, not a scarcity of food. In the viewpoint that follows, Lappé outlines the numerous changes in food production and policy that have occurred since the publication of her book as part of the "food movement" and contends that in nearly all phases of the process, from workers' rights to food production and marketing, improvements have been made. She applauds the increase in workers' wages, the growth in small farm and land ownership, the fight against seed patents and genetic modification of food, and the movement toward a more involved and fairer "agri-culture." She concludes that the food movement offers one of the best opportunities for people to take control of their lives and well-being and fight corporatism.*

For years I've been asked, "Since you wrote *Diet for a Small Planet* in 1971, have things gotten better or worse?" Hoping I don't sound glib, my response is always the same: "Both."

Frances Moore Lappé, "The Food Movement: Its Power and Possibilities," *Nation*, vol. 293, no. 14, October 3, 2011, pp. 11–12, 14–15. Copyright © 2011 by the Nation. All rights reserved. Reproduced by permission.

As food growers, sellers and eaters, we're moving in two directions at once.

The number of hungry people has soared to nearly 1 billion, despite strong global harvests. And for even more people, sustenance has become a health hazard—with the US diet implicated in four out of our top ten deadly diseases. Power over soil, seeds and food sales is ever more tightly held, and farmland in the global South [developing countries in the Southern Hemisphere] is being snatched away from indigenous people by speculators set to profit on climbing food prices. Just four companies control at least three-quarters of international grain trade; and in the United States, by 2000, just ten corporations—with boards totaling only 138 people—had come to account for half of US food and beverage sales. Conditions for American farmworkers remain so horrific that seven Florida growers have been convicted of slavery involving more than 1,000 workers. Life expectancy of US farmworkers is forty-nine years.

That's one current. It's antidemocratic and deadly.

There is, however, another current, which is democratizing power and aligning farming with nature's genius. Many call it simply "the global food movement." In the United States it's building on the courage of truth tellers from Upton Sinclair [an American author who wrote the novel *The Jungle* exposing the horrific working conditions in the meat packing industry in the early twentieth century] to Rachel Carson [an American conservationist and author of *Silent Spring*, a book credited with introducing environmentalism to the American public], and worldwide it has been gaining energy and breadth for at least four decades.

Some Americans see the food movement as "nice" but peripheral—a middle-class preoccupation with farmers' markets, community gardens and healthy school lunches. But no, I'll argue here. It is at heart revolutionary, with some of the world's poorest people in the lead, from Florida farmworkers to Indian villagers. It has the potential to transform not just the way we eat but the way we understand our world, including ourselves. And that vast power is just beginning to erupt.

Farmworkers Are Paid More

In a farmworker camp in Ohio, a young mother sat on her bed. She was dying of cancer, but with no bitterness she asked me a simple question: "We provide people food—why don't they respect our work?" That was 1984. She had no protection from pesticides, or even the right to safe drinking water in the field.

Twenty-five years later, in Immokalee, Florida, I walked through a grungy, sweltering 300-foot trailer, home to eight tomato pickers, but what struck me most was a sense of possibility in the workers themselves.

They are among the 4,000 mainly Latino, Mayan Indian and Haitian members of the Coalition of Immokalee Workers [CIW], formed in 1993—more than two decades after [labor activist] Cesar Chavez's United Farm Workers' victorious five-year grape strike and national boycott. In the 1990s, CIW's struggle over five years, including a 230-mile walk and hunger strike, achieved the first industrywide pay increase in twenty years. Still, it only brought real wages back to pre-1980 levels. So in 2001, CIW launched its Campaign for Fair Food. Dogged organizing forced four huge fast-food companies— McDonald's, Taco Bell, Burger King and Subway—to agree to pay a penny more per pound and adhere to a code of conduct protecting workers. Four large food-service providers, including Sodexo, were also brought on board. Beginning this fall [2011], CIW will start implementing these changes at 90 percent of Florida tomato farms—improving the lives of 30,000 tomato pickers. Now the campaign is focused on supermarkets such as Trader Joe's, Stop & Shop and Giant.

Market Share Has Increased

In Brazil, almost 400,000 farmworker families have not only found their voices but gained access to land, joining the roughly half-billion small farms worldwide that produce 70 percent of the world's food.

Elsewhere, calls for more equitable access to land in recent decades have generally gone nowhere—despite evidence that smallholders are typically more productive and better resource guardians than big operators.

So what happened in Brazil?

With the end of dictatorship in 1984 came the birth of arguably the largest social movement in the hemisphere: the Landless Workers Movement, known by its Portuguese acronym MST. Less than 4 percent of Brazil's landowners control about half the land, often gained illegally. MST's goal is land reform, and in 1988 Brazil's new Constitution gave the movement legal grounding: Article 5 states that "property shall fulfill its social function," and Article 184 affirms the government's power to "expropriate . . . for purposes of agrarian reform, rural property" that fails to meet this requirement. Well-organized occupations of unused land, under the cover of night, had been MST's early tactic; after 1988 the same approach helped compel the government to uphold the Constitution.

Because of the courage of these landless workers, a million people are building new lives on roughly 35 million acres, creating several thousand farming communities with schools serving 150,000 kids, along with hundreds of cooperative and other enterprises.

Nevertheless, MST co-founder João Pedro Stédile said early this year that the global financial crisis has led "international capitalists" to try to "protect their funds" by investing in Brazilian "land and energy projects"—driving renewed land concentration.

And in the United States? The largest 9 percent of farms produce more than 60 percent of output. But small farmers still control more than half our farmland, and the growing market for healthy fresh food has helped smallholders grow: their numbers went up by 18,467 between 2002 and 2007. To support them, last winter the Community Food Security Coalition held community "listening sessions," attended by 700 people, to sharpen citizen goals for the 2012 farm bill.

Seeds Can Be Patented

Just as dramatic is the struggle for the seed. More than 1,000 independent seed companies were swallowed up by multinationals in the past four decades, so today just three—Monsanto, DuPont and Syngenta—control about half the proprietary seed market worldwide.

Fueling the consolidation were three Supreme Court rulings since 1980—including one in 2002, with an opinion written by former Monsanto attorney Clarence Thomas—making it possible to patent life forms, including seeds. And in 1992 the Food and Drug Administration [FDA] released its policy on genetically modified organisms [GMOs], claiming that "the agency is not aware of any information showing that [GMO] foods ... differ from other foods in any meaningful or uniform way."

The government's green light fueled the rapid spread of GMOs and monopolies—so now most US corn and soybeans are GMO, with genes patented largely by one company: Monsanto. The FDA position helped make GMOs' spread so invisible that most Americans still don't believe they've ever eaten them—even though the grocery industry says they could be in 75 percent of processed food.

Even fewer Americans are aware that in 1999 attorney Steven Druker reported that in 40,000 pages of FDA files secured via a lawsuit, he found "memorandum after memorandum contain[ing] warnings about the unique hazards of genetically engineered food," including the possibility that they could contain "unexpected toxins, carcinogens or allergens."

The Fight Against Seed Patents

Yet at the same time, public education campaigns have succeeded in confining almost 80 percent of GMO planting to just three countries: the United States, Brazil and Argentina. In more than two dozen countries and in the European Union they've helped pass mandatory GMO labeling. Even China requires it.

In Europe, the anti-GMO tipping point came in 1999. Jeffrey Smith, author of *Seeds of Deception* [a book arguing that GMOs are dangerous], expects that the same shift will happen here, as more Americans than ever actively oppose GMOs. This year the "non-GMO" label is the third-fastest-growing new health claim on food packaging. Smith is also encouraged that milk products produced with the genetically modified drug rBGH "have been kicked out of Wal-Mart, Starbucks, Yoplait, Dannon, and most American dairies."

Around the world, millions are saying no to seed patenting as well. In homes and village seed banks, small farmers and gardeners are saving, sharing and protecting tens of thousands of seed varieties.

In the United States, the Seed Savers Exchange in Decorah, Iowa, estimates that since 1975 members have shared roughly a million samples of rare garden seeds.

In the Indian state of Andhra Pradesh—known as the pesticide capital of the world—a women-led village movement, the Deccan Development Society, puts seed-saving at the heart of its work. After the crushing failure of GMO cotton and ill health linked to pesticides, the movement has helped 125 villages convert to more nutritious, traditional crop mixes, feeding 50,000 people.

On a larger scale, [Indian environmental activist] Vandana Shiva's organization, Navdanya, has helped to free 500,000

This 2007 photograph shows Greenpeace's 200-foot crop circle in a Canadian corn field grown with Monsanto's NK603 genetically engineered seed, which has been linked to liver and kidney toxicity in rats. © AP Images/PRNewsFoto/Greenpeace.

farmers from chemical dependency and to save indigenous seeds—the group's learning and research center protects 3,000 varieties of rice, plus other crops.

Embracing Agri-Culture

In all these ways and more, the global food movement challenges a failing frame: one that defines successful agriculture and the solution to hunger as better technologies increasing yields of specific crops. This is typically called "industrial agriculture," but a better description might be "productivist," because it fixates on production, or "reductivist," because it narrows our focus to a single element.

Its near obsession with the yield of a monoculture is anti-ecological. It not only pollutes, diminishes and disrupts nature; it misses ecology's first lesson: relationships. Productivism isolates agriculture from its relational context—from its culture.

In 2008 a singular report helped crack the productivist frame. This report, "The International Assessment of Agricultural Knowledge, Science and Technology for Development" (known simply as IAASTD), explained that solutions to poverty, hunger and the climate crisis require agriculture that promotes producers' livelihoods, knowledge, resiliency, health and equitable gender relations, while enriching the natural environment and helping to balance the carbon cycle. Painstakingly developed over four years by 400 experts, the report has gained the support of more than fifty-nine governments, and even productivist strongholds like the World Bank.

IAASTD furthers an emerging understanding that agriculture can serve life only if it is regarded as a culture of healthy relationships, both in the field—among soil organisms, insects, animals, plants, water, sun—and in the human communities it supports: a vision lived by many indigenous people and captured in 1981 by [American farmer and writer] Wendell Berry in *The Gift of Good Land* and twenty years later by [British author] Jules Pretty in *Agri-Culture: Reconnecting People, Land and Nature.*

Across cultures, the global food movement is furthering agri-culture by uniting diverse actors and fostering democratic relationships. A leader is La Via Campesina, founded in 1993 when small farmers and rural laborers gathered from four continents in Belgium. Its goal is "food sovereignty"—a term carefully chosen to situate "those who produce, distribute, and consume food at the heart of food systems and policies, rather than the demands of markets and corporations," says the declaration closing the group's 2007 global gathering in Nyeleni, Mali. La Via Campesina connects 150 local and national organizations, and 200 million small farmers, in seventy countries. In 2009 it was included among civil society players on the UN Committee on Food Security.

And in the urban North [developed countries, mostly in the Northern Hemisphere], how is the food movement enhancing agri-culture?

For sure, more and more Americans are getting their hands in the dirt—motivated increasingly by a desire to cut "food miles" and greenhouse gases. Roughly a third of American households (41 million) garden, up 14 percent in 2009 alone. As neighbors join neighbors, community gardens are blooming. From only a handful in 1970, there are 18,000 community gardens today. In Britain community gardens are in such demand—with 100,000 Brits on waiting lists for a plot—that the mayor of London promised 2,012 new ones by 2012.

And in 2009 the Slow Food movement, with 100,000 members in 153 countries, created 300 "eat-ins"—shared meals in public space—to launch its US "Time for Lunch" campaign, with a goal of delicious healthy school meals for the 31 million kids eating them every day.

Shared Human Values

Agri-culture's unity of healthy farming ecology and social ecology transforms the market itself: from the anonymous, amoral selling and buying within a market structured to concentrate power to a market shaped by shared human values structured to ensure fairness and co-responsibility.

In 1965 British Oxfam created the first fair-trade organization, called Helping-by-Selling, in response to calls from poor countries for "trade, not aid." Today more than 800 products are fair-trade certified, directly benefiting 6 million people. Last year the US fair-trade market passed $1.5 billion.

The Real Food Challenge, launched by young people in 2007, is working to jump-start a US swing to "real food"—defined as that respecting "human dignity and health, animal welfare, social justice and environmental sustainability." Student teams are mobilizing to persuade campus decisionmakers to commit themselves to making a minimum of 20 percent of their college or university food "real" by 2020. With more than 350 schools already on board, the Challenge founders have set an ambitious goal: to shift $1 billion to real food purchases in ten years.

Farmers' markets, the direct exchange between farmer and eater, are also creating a fairer agri-culture. So rare before the mid-'90s that the USDA [US Department of Agriculture] didn't even bother to track them, more than 7,000 farmers' markets dot the country in 2011, a more than fourfold increase in seventeen years.

Other democratic economic models are also gaining ground:

In 1985 an irrepressible Massachusetts farmer named Robyn Van En helped create the first US Community Supported Agriculture (CSA) program, in which eaters are no longer just purchasers but partners, helping to shoulder the farmer's risk by prepaying for a share of the harvest before the planting season. On weekends, "my" CSA—Waltham Fields, near Boston—is alive as families pick and chat, and kids learn how to spot the yummiest strawberries. Now there are 2,500 CSAs across the country, while more than 12,500 farms informally use this prepay, partnership approach.

The cooperative model is spreading too, replacing one dollar, one vote—the corporate form—with one person, one vote. In the 1970s, US food cooperatives took off. Today there are 160 nationwide, and co-op veteran Annie Hoy in Ashland, Oregon, sees a new upsurge. Thirty-nine have just opened, or are "on their way right now," she told me.

Funky storefronts of the 1970s, famous for limp organic carrots, have morphed into mouthwatering community hubs. Beginning as a food-buying club of fifteen families in 1953, Seattle's PCC Natural Markets has nine stores and almost 46,000 members, making it the largest US food cooperative. Its sales more than doubled in a decade.

Producer co-ops have also made huge gains. In 1988 a handful of worried farmers, watching profits flow to middlemen, not to them, launched the Organic Valley Family of Farms. Today Organic Valley's more than 1,600 farmer owners span thirty-two states, generating sales of more than $500 million in 2008.

New Rules

The global food system reflects societies' rules—often uncodified—that determine who eats and how our earth fares. In the United States, rules increasingly reflect our nation's slide into "privately held government." But in rule-setting, too, energy is hardly unidirectional.

In 1999, on the streets of Seattle, 65,000 environmentalists, labor and other activists made history, blunting the antidemocratic agenda of the World Trade Organization. In 2008 more citizens than ever engaged in shaping the farm bill, resulting in rules encouraging organic production. The movement has also established 100 "food policy councils"—new local-to-state, multi-stakeholder coordinating bodies. And this year, eighty-three plaintiffs joined the Public Patent Foundation in suing Monsanto, challenging its GMO seeds' "usefulness" (required for patenting) as well as the company's right to patent seeds to begin with.

Even small changes in the rules can create huge possibilities. Consider, for example, the ripples from a 2009 Brazilian law requiring at least 30 percent of school meals to consist of food from local family farms.

Rules governing rights are the human community's foundational guarantees to one another—and the [UN's] 1948 Universal Declaration of Human Rights gave access to food that status. Since then, nearly two dozen nations have planted the right to food in their constitutions. If you wonder whether it matters, note that when Brazil undertook a multifaceted "zero hunger" campaign, framing food as a right, the country slashed its infant death rate by about a third in seven years.

Breaking the Spell of Corporatism

This rising global food movement taps universal human sensibilities—expressed in Hindu farmers in India saving seeds, Muslim farmers in Niger turning back the desert and Christian farmers in the United States practicing biblically inspired Creation Care. In these movements lies the revolutionary power of the food movement: its capacity to upend a life-destroying belief system that has brought us power-concentrating corporatism.

Corporatism, after all, depends on our belief in the fairy tale that market "magic" ([former president] Ronald Reagan's unforgettable term) works on its own without us.

Food can break that spell. For the food movement's power is that it can shift our sense of self: from passive, disconnected consumers in a magical market to active, richly connected co-producers in societies we are creating—as share owners in a CSA farm or purchasers of fair-trade products or actors in public life shaping the next farm bill.

The food movement's power is connection itself. Corporatism distances us from one another, from the earth—and even from our own bodies, tricking them to crave that which destroys them—while the food movement celebrates our reconnection. Years ago in Madison, Wisconsin, CSA farmer Barb Perkins told me about her most rewarding moments: "Like in town yesterday," she said, "I saw this little kid, wide-eyed, grab his mom's arm and point at me. 'Mommy,' he said. 'Look. There's our farmer!'"

At its best, this movement encourages us to "think like an ecosystem," enabling us to see a place for ourselves connected to all others, for in ecological systems "there are no parts, only participants," German physicist Hans Peter Duerr reminds us. With an "eco-mind" we can see through the productivist fixation that inexorably concentrates power, generating scarcity for some, no matter how much we produce. We're freed from the premise of lack and the fear it feeds. Aligning food and farming with nature's genius, we realize there's more than enough for all.

As the food movement stirs, as well as meets, deep human needs for connection, power and fairness, let's shed any notion that it's simply "nice" and seize its true potential to break the spell of our disempowerment.

The Local Food Movement Will Revolutionize the Food Industry

John Ikerd

John Ikerd is a professor of agriculture and applied economics at the University of Missouri, Columbia. He has researched and written extensively about the economics of sustainable farming in the United States.

What began as a countercultural movement started by hippies in the 1960s, the natural food movement grew into an organic food movement and eventually the local food movement of today, according to Ikerd. In the following viewpoint, Ikerd traces the evolution of this movement and argues that the modern American consumer prefers food that comes from a local source—either a local co-op that buys from local producers or a farmer who sells the goods directly to the consumer without a middle man. This new consumer drive, in the author's view, has resulted from increased knowledge about the health detriments of modern food production techniques that emphasize high yield over quality and a disillusionment with industrialized agriculture. Ikerd believes that this new consumer consciousness holds the promise of pushing American society to become healthier and revolutionizing the production and consumption of food in the United States.

On March 26, 2010 Jamie Oliver, an outspoken British chef turned activist, called for a "food revolution" in America. The occasion was the premier of a six-episode reality show on ABC Television. The show was filmed in Huntington,

John Ikerd, "Local Food: Revolution and Reality," Prepared Presentation for the Biennial Conference of the United States Agricultural Information Network, Agriculture Without Borders, Lafayette, IN, May 11, 2010.

West Virginia—supposedly the unhealthiest city in the unhealthiest country in the world. The premise of the show is that people's physical health is linked directly to the foods they eat. Obesity, diabetes, hypertension, heart disease, and many forms of cancer—epidemic in America—have all been linked directly to diet.

In the first episode, Oliver pointed out that today's children are the first generation whose members are expected to live shorter lives than their parents. It's not the kids' fault; they eat what parents and other adults choose to feed them, or at least allow them to eat. Too often, this means whatever is cheapest, quickest, and most convenient. Over the past few decades, health care spending in the U.S. has raised to almost double the amount spent for food, which is not likely a coincidence. In the pursuit of quick, convenient, cheap food, Americans have become the most overfed and undernourished people in the world. It's time for a "food revolution."

Actually, the food revolution was well underway long before Jamie Oliver arrived in West Virginia. Health and nutrition are but the latest motivations for rejecting the "food-like substances" that dominate today's industrial, global, corporately controlled food system. The local food movement is most visible in the U.S. In a 2008 food industry study, sales of local foods were estimated to have grown from $4 billion in 2002 to $5 billion in 2007 and were projected to reach $11 billion by 2011. Organic food sales are still far larger, more than $20 billion, but local foods have replaced organic foods as the most dynamic sector of the retail food market.

The Food Movement Grows

The local food movement has its roots in the natural food movement of the 1960s, which began with the "back to the earth" people dropping out of the American mainstream and forming their own communities or "communes." Rachel Carson's 1962 book, *Silent Spring*, had awakened public awareness to the environmental risks of agricultural pesticides. The "hippies" responded by producing their own *natural* foods, buying natural foods at local farmers markets, and establishing the first cooperatively owned and operated natural food stores. Most knew where their natural food came from because they knew the farmers who grew it. To these early natural food advocates, *organic* was more a way of life as a way to grow good, healthy food. It was a rejection of the mechanistic way of thinking that supported industrial development, including industrial agriculture.

During the 1970s and 1980s, the natural food movement spread far beyond the hippie communities, as more people became aware of the food safety and environmental risks associated with industrial agriculture. The growing market for natural foods laid the foundation for a booming market in organic foods during the 1990s. As natural food retailers took a larger share of the natural foods market, fewer consumers then knew the farmers who grew their food so they needed some other means of knowing that their food was grown naturally. *Organic* certification was a means of assuring consumers that legitimate standards for *natural* food production had been followed. Organic farmers across the U.S. formed organizations to define organic standards and to inspect organic farms to verify compliance. Organic certification allowed producers to gain access to even more distant markets, as farmers and consumers began to rely on certification rather than personal relationships.

The late '80s and early '90s brought dramatic changes in organic foods retailing. By the late '80s, several natural foods retailers had expanded into small chain store operations, operating from three to 20 stores. In 1991, Whole Foods, then a six-store operation, began buying out other natural food stores, beginning a consolidation process that ultimately would reshape the natural foods market. In 1993, Wild Oats followed the lead of Whole Foods and began acquiring other natural foods cooperatives and small retail chains. The share of the organic market held by *independent* natural foods and health foods stores fell from 62% in 1998 to 31% in 2003. Total sales of organic foods grew an average rate of 20% per year during the 1990s and well into the 2000s, doubling every three to four years. . . .

From Organic to Local

In 2002, the USDA [US Department of Agriculture] launched its national program for certification of organic foods. However, uniform national standards actually facilitated the ongoing industrialization of organic food production and distribution—the specialization, standardization, and consolidation of control needed to accommodate the mainstream food system. With greater standardization, organic producers continued to specialize and consolidate into even larger scale operations. Large producers typically could meet these *minimum* requirements at lower costs than could the philosophically committed organic farmers. This industrialization of organics left smaller independent organic farmers and natural foods coops struggling for their economic survival.

However, many discriminating natural foods consumers were already moving beyond organic to *local*. They didn't trust either the corporate food system or the government to maintain the integrity of either conventional or organic foods. Many people in the new food movement didn't trust certified organic; they wanted to buy their foods locally from people they knew and trusted. If you asked these people why they prefer local foods they would probably mention freshness and flavor. However, the local food movement today is about far more than a search for fresh and flavorful foods; it's about a search for food with integrity.

The Chefs Collaborative, a network of more than 1,000 American chefs, promotes the "joys of local, seasonal, and artisanal cooking," proclaiming that "cultural and biological diversity are essential for the health of the earth and its inhabitants." These same cultural and ethical values are reflected in the Slow Food movement, a worldwide organization with about 85,000 members in over 100 countries. Their website states, "We believe that the food we eat should taste good; that it should be produced in a clean way that does not harm the environment, animal welfare or our health; that food producers should receive fair compensation for their work, and that all people should have access to good clean food." *Good, clean,* and *fair* are becoming the watchwords of the local foods movement.

Local Foods More Nutritious

The natural food movement is being fueled today by scientific studies indicating that nutritive values of foods have declined with the industrialization of the food system, verifying Jamie Oliver's insinuations. One prominent academic study compared nutrient levels in 43 garden crops in 1999 with levels documented in benchmark nutrient studies conducted by USDA in 1950. The scientists found declines in median concentrations of six important nutrients: protein -6%, calcium -16%, phosphorus -9%, iron -15%, riboflavin -38%, and vitamin C -2%. Another study published in the *Journal of Applied Nutrition* in 1993 showed nutritional deficiencies for conventional foods relative to organic foods. Organically grown apples, potatoes, pears, wheat, and sweet corn, purchased over a two-year period, averaged 63% higher in calcium, 73% higher in iron, 118% higher in magnesium, 91% higher in phosphorus, 125% higher in potassium, and 60% higher in zinc than conventional foods purchased at the same time.

Other studies have shown that yield-enhancing technologies—fertilizers, pesticides, plant density, and irrigation— reduce the nutrient content of field crops by amounts generally consistent with the results for the 50-year nutrient declines and differences between conventional and organic crops. These

A woman holds a basket of peaches at a farmers market in Richmond, Virginia. © Ariel Skelley/Blend Images/Alamy.

results should come as no surprise to anyone who understands that industrial agriculture derives profits primarily from *quantity* factors: acres farmed, head produced, yields per acre, rates of gain, and the cost efficiency of large-scale production. *Quality* factors affecting prices typically are incidental to profits and are often associated with cosmetic appearance rather than nutrition. . . .

Local Movement Goes Viral

There is no scarcity of information today on the subject of food. . . .

[Books and documentaries] all tell the same story of a food system that is lacking in ecological, social, and economic integrity.

These books and documentaries also tell a story of hope for the future through the voices and images of the farmers and consumers who are creating a new, sustainable food system. The farmers may label themselves organic, biodynamic, ecological, natural, holistic, or choose no label at all; but they were all pursuing the same basic purpose. They are creating systems of farming that can maintain their productivity and usefulness to society indefinitely—a permanent, sustainable agriculture. They are producing food with ecological, social, and economic integrity.

The stories tend to focus on a few celebrity farmers, such as Joel Salatin (*Polyface Farms, Inc.*) of Swope, VA and Will Allen (*Growing Power Inc.*) of Milwaukee, WI. However, there are tens of thousands of these new farmers scattered across the country. At least six "sustainable agriculture" conferences in the U.S. and Canada draw 1,500 to 2,500 people each year. Those attending include farm families and their customers and friends. Conferences drawing 500 to 700 people are becoming almost commonplace and virtually every state in the U.S. has an organic or sustainable agriculture organization, most hosting conferences that draw 100 to 250 people annually. The modern sustainable agriculture movement, which began with the "back to the earth" movement of the 1960s, is spreading like a virus through American agriculture.

The tens-of-thousands of new sustainable farmers are supported by tens of millions of consumers who are searching for alternatives to the industrial foods they find in today's supermarkets and fast food franchises. Food industry studies indicate approximately one-third of American consumers are willing pay premium prices for healthful and nutritious foods that have ecological, social, and economic integrity. Many are turning to local farmers and local markets to ensure the integrity of their food. The local foods movement has been doubling the number of farmers markets each decade, even as organic foods moved into mainstream supermarkets.

Retailers and Institutions Go Local

People tend to underestimate the importance of the local food movement because they associate local with home farmers markets and community supported agricultural organizations or CSAs, and more recently, home and community gardens. While farmers markets and CSAs have been growing rapidly, they still account for a very small portion of total food sales. The number of home vegetable gardens also exploded after the sharp run up in food prices during 2008—including one at the White House. While farmers markets, CSAs, and gardens are and will continue to be important, the local food movement is probably most accurately defined by the growing number of retail food stores and institutional food buyers who are committed to sourcing as much food as possible from local growers. . . .

The local food revolution is also moving into institutional markets—schools, hospitals, extended care facilities, etc.—in addition to supermarkets and restaurants. The most impressive progress thus far seems to have been made in getting sustainably produced local foods into public schools. For example, more than 500 public school districts and 95 colleges and universities currently have active programs to provide U.S. students with locally grown foods. By the way, Jamie Oliver started his food revolution in Huntington by getting nutritious food into the local schools of Huntington.

Supermarkets and institutional markets will continue to be important. However, the food systems of the future may more closely resemble today's multi-farm CSAs. Grown Locally, Idaho's Bounty, and the Oklahoma Food Cooperative, for example, are cooperative organizations of farmers that offer a variety of vegetables, fruits, meats, eggs, cheese, baked goods, flowers, and herbs produced by local farmers. Many items are available as CSA shares, standing orders, or for week-by-week purchase. Customers may have the option of on-farm pick-up, local delivery points, or delivery to the door for an added charge. Websites allow producers to post what they have available each week, ensuring that products sold are available for delivery and allowing customers to place or revise their orders on the website. . . .

A Food Revolution

This is the current reality of the local food movement. The total sales of all alternative foods—natural, organic, local . . .— probably still amount to something less than 10% of total retail food sales. However, the natural food movement is still less than fifty years old and was virtually unknown until about 20 years ago. The movement has grown tremendously over the past two decades and continues to grow, in spite of the economic recession. It will only take the right spark at the right time to ignite an explosion in public *demand* for "good food." Jamie Oliver came to America at time when the country was ripe for revolution. It remains to be seen whether his television show will be the spark many Americans have been waiting and hoping for. Regardless, today's reality is that local food is moving us ever closer to a food revolution.

Will the Food Safety Modernization Act Help Prevent Outbreaks of Foodborne Illness?

Michael R. Taylor

Michael R. Taylor is the deputy commissioner for foods at the US Food and Drug Administration.

On January 4, 2011, President Barack Obama signed the Food Safety Modernization Act (FSMA) into law. This legislation was created to update the methods used by the Food and Drug Administration (FDA) to ensure that the US food supply remains free of viruses, bacteria, and other microbes that cause foodborne illness. In the following viewpoint, Taylor argues that the FSMA will provide the necessary tools to improve food safety in the United States. He highlights the importance of many provisions in the act that will aid food safety personnel in securing US food products. Specifically, he points to the emphasis on prevention rather than reaction to problems, the focus on inspection and quality assurance of national and international food suppliers, and the integration of food safety systems on the local, state, and national levels. With this mandate to improve food safety, Taylor believes that the FSMA provides the country with the opportunity to craft an improved, modern system of food safety management.

Large-scale outbreaks of foodborne illness have recently focused attention on the ability of the U.S. food-safety system to protect the public health. The nationwide outbreak of

Michael R. Taylor, "Will the Food Safety Modernization Act Help Prevent Outbreaks of Foodborne Illness?" *New England Journal of Medicine*, vol. 365, no. 9, September 1, 2011, pp. e18 (1–3). Copyright © 2011 by Massachusetts Medical Society. All rights reserved. Reproduced by permission.

Salmonella enterica serotype Typhimurium infection associated with peanut products that is described by Cavallero et al. is one example. This contamination, which was ultimately traced to the Peanut Corporation of America (PCA), took a high toll—714 people were affected, about 200 were hospitalized, and 9 died. Investigators found multiple potential routes of contamination at PCA facilities, such as rain leakage and cross-contamination between raw and roasted peanuts. Although the outbreak was eventually contained, key parts of the food-safety system clearly failed.

There is a public health imperative to do better. The burden of foodborne illness is substantial: about 1 in 6 people in the United States get sick each year, 128,000 are hospitalized, and about 3000 die. We know that foodborne illness is not just a mild annoyance—it can lead to lifelong chronic diseases, such as arthritis and renal failure, and can cause death. Moreover, outbreaks can reduce consumers' confidence in the food supply and cause major economic disruptions for the food system.

Ensuring food safety is a difficult job. A global marketplace provides a diverse array of food products. Many processed foods are manufactured through complex technology. New strains of *Escherichia coli* are emerging—such as the O104:H4 strain in the recent German outbreak—and we're seeing unexpected pathogens in some food items, such as salmonella in nuts. Given our complex food-distribution channels, it's not easy to trace contaminated products to their source rapidly.

The challenge is great, but we believe we have a historic opportunity to reduce foodborne illness under the new Food Safety Modernization Act (FSMA). Enacted on January 4, 2011, the FSMA gives the Food and Drug Administration (FDA) a modern mandate and toolkit to improve the safety of the country's food supply.

Most fundamentally, the law clarifies that people and businesses that provide food to the public, whether they produce, process, transport, or sell food, are responsible for taking the steps necessary to ensure that they've identified and controlled hazards that could make food unsafe. Though most companies take proper precautions, it takes only one uncontrolled situation to cause an outbreak. The FDA's core job under the FSMA is to set modern prevention-oriented standards and ensure high rates of compliance. Consumers have a responsibility to ensure food safety by properly handling, preparing, and storing food, but they should not be responsible for correcting mistakes that were made earlier in the farm-to-table chain.

The FSMA shifts our food-safety focus from reaction and response to prevention, so that prudent preventive measures will be systematically built into all parts of the food system. The law directs the FDA to issue a rule requiring comprehensive preventive controls for most facilities. In the future, each facility will have to produce a written analysis identifying the hazards associated with the foods it handles and the processes used to manufacture them. The required documentation will describe the controls the facility has implemented to prevent the identified hazards, including a plan for monitoring the controls and correcting problems when failures occur.

Preventive controls are not new in the food industry; many companies already employ them, and the FDA already requires them for foods such as juices, seafood, and shell eggs. But Congress has given the FDA an explicit mandate to use the tool more broadly. Details of the new requirements under the FSMA will be developed through the rulemaking process, and the public will have the opportunity to provide input (more information can be found at www.fda.gov/fsma).

The new law has provisions to help ensure that food from abroad is as safe as food produced domestically. Our food supply is global, with 15% coming from other countries, and the percentage is higher for certain commodities: 75% of our seafood, 20% of our vegetables, and 50% of our fruit is imported. The FSMA mandates a new safety system that makes importers accountable for verifying that the required controls are in place in foreign food facilities that export products to the United States. The FDA will continue to conduct electronic risk-based screening of all food shipments before they arrive in the country and conduct further analyses at the port of entry when warranted. But the requirement that importers perform verification activities will boost our assurance that imported food is safe.

The FSMA also provides the FDA with new inspection and enforcement tools to ensure that companies are carrying out their responsibilities and to keep contaminated products from reaching the marketplace. With the help of its state partners and others, the FDA will conduct more frequent and targeted inspections that will include verification that facilities are properly implementing preventive controls. We will have access to facilities' food-safety plans and the records they will be required to keep to document their implementation. With the FSMA's broad prevention framework, we will be able to develop new inspection approaches that better target facilities and products on the basis of risk. When a company fails to voluntarily recall unsafe food, the FDA has new authority to issue a mandatory recall. The law also gives the FDA more authority to prevent the release into the marketplace of adulterated or misbranded food, including potentially harmful food. In addition, if a food producer in another country does not permit the FDA to inspect its facility, the agency can refuse to allow food from that facility into the United States.

The FSMA also gives the Centers for Disease Control and Prevention new responsibilities to enhance federal, state, and local surveillance systems for foodborne illness so that we can identify and control outbreaks more quickly while gaining the scientific knowledge to prevent future ones. The FSMA implicitly recognizes the importance of good data to drive evidence-based interventions that could reduce illnesses. State and local health departments are responsible for a large proportion of these activities, and we must provide them with resources to do their job with modern methods.

Finally, we have a mandate from Congress to work more closely with our government partners at the federal, state, local, territorial, and tribal level. Our goal is to establish an integrated, nationwide food-safety system with harmonized inspections, requirements, surveillance methods, and training. The FSMA also includes similar directives to work with and help build the capacity of our counterparts in other countries.

The law calls for a new food-safety system—one that makes better use of public and private resources to prevent food-safety problems. Implementation will take time. Some provisions are already in place, but many others require rulemaking, which will ensure that we get input from all our stakeholders and that the regulations we issue are well thought out and practical for the diverse businesses that will be affected.

Implementation also requires investment in the science that can illuminate hazards and ways of preventing them, retraining of FDA field staff in new inspection methods, capacity building that enables us to leverage state resources, and the construction of a new import-safety system that meets the challenges of our globalized food supply.

The FSMA represents an opportunity to build a system that can prevent many outbreaks of foodborne illness and reduce the public health impact of those that do occur. We expect to better meet high consumer expectations and enhance the food system's economic viability. We will be working with stakeholders, with Congress, and with the administration to ensure that the FDA has the necessary resources to implement this landmark legislation.

Increased Regulation Under the Food Safety Modernization Act Will Have Unintended Negative Consequences

Gary Wolensky, Anne Marie Ellis, and Kelly Regan

Gary Wolensky, Anne Marie Ellis, and Kelly Regan are attorneys with Hewitt Wolesnky LLP, a law firm in Newport Beach, California, concerned with product liability litigation.

Following the passage of the Food Safety Modernization Act (FSMA) in January 2011, many praised the legislation's potential to improve the ability of the Food and Drug Administration (FDA) to ensure the safety of the American food supply. In the viewpoint that follows, however, Wolensky, Ellis, and Regan argue that the FSMA's breadth and lack of specificity could result in unforeseen negative consequences that could not only limit the act's effectiveness but also present new problems for food producers and consumers. For example, the authors point out that the sweeping authority granted to the FDA in its ability to issue mandatory recalls of potentially harmful food products and access corporate records could lead overzealous lawyers and consumers to file liability suits seeking punitive damages against food companies. In addition to increasing the probability of lawsuits against producers, the authors believe that this legislation makes food transporters and restaurants vulnerable to similar types of legislation. Further, the authors charge that the legisla-

Gary Wolensky, Anne Marie Ellis, and Kelly Regan, "The Food Safety Modernization Act: Another Law of Unintended Consequences?" *Mass Torts*, vol. 10, no. 1, Fall 2011.

tion fails in its attempt to make state and federal food regulation more uniform and could in the end succeed only in increasing the cost of food for consumers.

On January 4, 2011, President [Barack] Obama signed the Food Safety Modernization Act (FSMA) into law. This law represents the most sweeping change to the U.S. food safety system in more than 70 years. The new legislation was prompted in part by the recent high-profile outbreaks of food poisoning in the United States. The U.S. Centers for Disease Control and Prevention estimates that one out of every six Americans contracts a food-borne illness every year, or about 48 million people annually. Of those, an estimated 128,000 people will be hospitalized, and 3,000 will die each year. The underlying goal of the FSMA is to enable the Food and Drug Administration (FDA) to better protect public health by ensuring the safety and security of the food supply. It is intended to allow the FDA to focus more on preventing food safety problems rather than reacting to problems after they occur. Is this another poorly-thought-out law, such as the Consumer Product Safety Improvement Act and the health care legislation? Or is it designed to accomplish its intended purpose? . . .

Unintended Consequences

Although the underlying goal of the FSMA is to enable the FDA to better protect public health by ensuring the safety and security of the food supply, the practical effects of the FSMA are that it is costly, that it applies to essentially any entity in the food industry, that it is uncertain, that it gives the FDA sweeping new enforcement authorities, and that it will likely create a whole host of litigation issues. Mid-sized business are expected to bear the greatest burden, because large food facilities are likely to be already strictly monitoring the safety of food they produce, and small businesses are exempt from many of the requirements. Moreover, funding for the act (estimated at $1.4 billion over five years) still has to be approved. However, the FDA is moving forward with implementation based on existing resources and the assumption that the necessary additional funding will ultimately be provided.

Does this sound familiar? Here is another piece of legislation that has a laudable goal but that results in onerous, poorly-thought-out regulations that create unintended economic consequences on businesses struggling in the worst economic times that this nation has seen in decades. Indeed, this has become an all too familiar pattern that will likely result in billions of dollars in compliance costs to the food industry, leading to layoffs, bankruptcies, and business closures. We remember what Congress did in an effort to protect children from lead products imported from China. The Consumer Products Safety Improvement Act of 2008 [which imposed new requirements on wide-ranging businesses] turned into a nightmare for industry as well as the Consumer Products Safety Commission, as it was so poorly drafted and so overbroad in relation to the problem it was intended to address that it cost the industry billions of dollars to comply with it. That statute assumed that children would eat lead out of bicycle brakes. . . .

Too Far-Reaching

One of the most ominous and far-reaching provisions of the FSMA is the FDA's new mandatory recall authority. The FDA issues general information about all new recalls it is monitoring through a weekly publication, *Enforcement Report*. As it relates to product liability law, this authority is noteworthy because it enables the FDA to initiate a mandatory recall campaign when a company fails to remove unsafe food from the market voluntarily.

The FDA may issue a recall under section 206, after determining "that there is a reasonable probability that an article of food is adulterated . . . or misbranded . . . and the use or exposure ... will cause serious adverse health consequences or death to humans or animals." The FDA must provide the company the opportunity to cease distribution voluntarily and recall the affected product. If a company fails to do so, the FDA can order it immediately to cease distribution. Following the order, the FDA will provide the responsible party an opportunity for an informal hearing within two days. Failure to comply with the recall order is a prohibited act and the responsible party may be subject to civil penalties. In addition, to make FDA recalls more transparent, the agency must, within 90 days after the date of enactment, update its website so that users can search for all information related to the recall, including the status of the recall. With the ability to access this information at any moment and to identify companies undergoing a recall, plaintiffs and their attorneys can quickly and more easily identify potential defendants and file suit against the recalling company. Therefore, companies should have a strong product recall plan in place to minimize potential injury to consumers and to the company, and they should maintain effective relationships with the media and regulatory agencies.

Needless Litigation Could Result

Given the FDA's authority to order a recall under section 206 if it determines a food facility's products have a "reasonable probability of causing serious adverse health consequences"— not that such consequences are "more likely than not"—there is a high probability that plaintiffs will attempt to use this finding to make the inferential leap that a company's products are unreasonably dangerous and subject the company to product liability litigation. To recover under a strict product liability theory, a plaintiff need only show that a product was defective in manufacture or design, that the manufacturer failed to adequately warn of the product's risks, or that the product breached a warranty. Plaintiffs will undoubtedly attempt to make the stealth preemption argument that if a food has been identified by FDA as causing serious adverse health consequences or risk of death, it is "defective" and breached express and implied warranties.

Furthermore, those companies that refuse to issue a voluntary recall and that are subject to a mandatory recall by the FDA, could find themselves subject to product liability claims for failure to warn. To establish a failure to warn claim, a plaintiff must show that a product is defective because of inadequate instructions or warnings when the foreseeable risks of harm posed by the product could have been reduced or avoided by proper instructions. If companies fail to issue warnings on their own, plaintiffs will likely argue these companies failed to warm consumers of the dangers in their products. Thus, the no-fault scheme of strict product liability may be exploited by eager plaintiffs upon implementation of these new regulations.

Similarly, pursuant to section 207 of the FSMA, the FDA now has the power to administratively detain food when the agency has "reason to believe an article of food is adulterated or misbranded." This standard lowers the bar for the FDA to use administrative detention. Foods detained by FDA are also likely candidates for negligence and product liability claims, as plaintiffs will likely argue that foods labeled "adulterated" or "misbranded" necessarily breach the standard of care to provide consumers with food safe for consumption. "Adulterated" and "misbranded" might as well read "defective" for purposes of product liability claims, even though, again, the FDA's administrative standards are far more lax than what the common law requires.

Increased Records Access

Under the FSMA, the FDA has greater access to company records than ever before. Prior to the passage of the FSMA, the FDA could access records relating only to articles of food believed to be adulterated. Now, where there is a "reasonable belief" that an article of food is adulterated, the FDA may request not only the records of the affected food but also the records of any other article of food that FDA reasonably believes is "likely to be affected in a similar manner." Furthermore, the FDA is entitled to access "any records needed to assist" its determination of whether a food is adulterated. Thus, a company must not only produce records of a food believed to be adulterated but also provide the records of foods that may be similarly affected.

With the FDA's new ability to request records of foods it believes may be similarly affected, plaintiffs have access to records never before released on such a wide scale. Under the Freedom of Information Act, plaintiffs will likely be able to access the documents amassed by FDA. The expanded records access opens the door to numerous possibilities for private litigation, and it also has the potential to provide plaintiffs with claims for punitive damages.

Claims for punitive damages require a showing of malice, oppression, or fraud. To make this showing, the plaintiffs must prove that the defendants acted with intent to cause injury or with a willful and knowing disregard of the rights or safety of another. Under the expanded records access, companies are required to produce all documents relating to the affected food, including all records relating to the manufacture, processing, packing, distribution, receipt, holding, or importation of the food product. Plaintiffs may now have access to records that they will be sure to claim reflect intent to cause injury or knowing disregard for the safety of consumers, which led to the contamination of the food product, allowing them to make a claim for punitive damages. Further, the documents could be used by plaintiffs to allege that the company had "knowledge" of contaminated food, which also may prove helpful in making a claim for punitive damages. Where a plaintiff can show that a company knowingly engaged in unsafe practices, the plaintiff may be more inclined to assert a claim for punitive damages. . . .

Unaligned State and Federal Policies

The FSMA does not have an express preemption clause prohibiting concurrent food safety regulation under state law. The act contains "no preemption" provisions in sections 103, 105, 112, and 402. Food companies must therefore be mindful of liability under state laws while complying with the FSMA. An example of potentially conflicting state laws is found in the Minnesota statutes. Those statutes permit state personnel to inspect facilities in Minnesota to enforce the Minnesota food laws. These inspections occur much more frequently than inspections that will be required under the FSMA. Thus, food facilities in Minnesota will continue to be inspected far more frequently under Minnesota law than under the FSMA. While the FSMA may give the appearance of creating uniform standards in food safety regulation, food companies must continue to monitor and abide by state-imposed regulations.

Others Could Be Affected

The FSMA may also permit plaintiffs to add new categories of defendants to lawsuits that they may not have considered, or even had a cause of action against, in the past. Companies involved in the transportation of food products may be one such category of new defendants added to the list, as they will soon be required to comply with FDA-established rules ensuring the "sanitary transportation of food." Section 111 of the FSMA instructs the FDA to establish rules that require persons engaged in the transportation of food to use sanitary transportation practices. The regulation provides little guidance with respect to what practices will be considered "sanitary." At this point, one can only guess what regulations the FDA may come up with, and until rules are established, those involved in food transportation will have little direction other than knowing they must adhere to the vague concept of "sanitary transportation of food."

Under the current standards, restaurants and retailers remain largely unaffected by the FSMA. None of the provisions in the FSMA will have an immediate or direct impact on restaurants. However, restaurants may be subject to the enhanced tracking and tracing of food and record keeping. These regulations aim to decrease the reaction time in case of an outbreak of food-borne illness. In addition, restaurants that import directly from foreign countries will be subject to the regulations on imported foods. However, restaurants, like producers and manufacturers, should pay close attention to their food suppliers and prepare themselves to manage the recall process effectively. A recall initiated by a supplier could lead to increased costs and possibly a shortage of popular menu items, thus interrupting a restaurant's business. At the same time, restaurants should have their own recall plans in place to ensure that recalls are effectively communicated among the staff so that possibly contaminated food is not served. . . .

Increased Food Cost and Litigation

Although the FSMA aims to enact the most sweeping changes to the United States' approach to food safety, its future is far from certain. The FDA faces significant funding hurdles to implement the proposed regulations unless Congress reexamines the breadth and underlying implications of the act. Necessary funding will be provided for its implementation and enforcement. The future for food companies remains unknown, and Americans will continue to watch to see what effects the FSMA has on U.S. food safety, the food industry, and the cost of food. Undoubtedly, the uncontrollable increase in industry costs under onerous regulations will be passed on to the public. Finally, the FSMA has great potential to increase exponentially the number of consumer claims and lawsuits against all those involved in the food industry.

For Further Discussion

1. George Ritzer in Chapter 2, discussing *Fast Food Nation* shortly after its publication in 2001, maintains that the book presents an accurate depiction of the ways in which all links in the food production chain—from farmers to fast food restaurant workers—had to alter their practices to fulfill the fast food industry's demand for speed. Reread this viewpoint and then reread the viewpoint in Chapter 3 by John Ikerd about the local food movement, written in 2010, not even a full decade after the publication of *Fast Food Nation*. In it, Ikerd contends that Americans have increasingly begun to favor locally produced foods. Do you believe that the local movement described by Ikerd presents a credible threat to the fast food industry and its practices? Has the culture changed significantly since the publication of *Fast Food Nation* from one focused on food that can be prepared and consumed quickly to one more concerned about relationships with food and food producers? If so, how great is the change, and do you think it will continue? Cite examples from the essays to support your view.

2. The viewpoints in Chapter 2 by Andrew Engelson and Madhu Suri Prakash and Dana L. Stuchul highlight the ways in which the book *Fast Food Nation* could incite readers to demand change in the food industry. In Chapter 3, Frances Moore Lappé points out some of the positive changes that have occurred since the publication of her 1971 book about the problems with food production. On the basis of these readings do you think Eric Schlosser's book could result in changes similar to those described by Lappé? Why or why not? Use specific examples of the changes that are possible from the readings and carefully support your claims.

3. The viewpoints by Gary Alan Fine and Steven A. Shaw in the second chapter deal with the ways in which consumers in the free market impact how companies conduct business. Reread these essays and consider the interplay between consumer demand and business's response. How much control do consumers have in the current system? With regard to the fast food industry, can consumer demand for healthier food cause these companies to offer healthier choices? Incorporate quotes from the viewpoints as well as your own examples into your answer.

4. The final two viewpoints in Chapter 2 examine two films based on the ideas and information presented in *Fast Food Nation*. Keeping in mind that the article by Dave Hoskin is a critique of the fictionalized version of the book and the second article is an interview with the director of the documentary based on some of the book's ideas, determine which genre, fiction or documentary, you think would be a better vehicle to present the ideas of *Fast Food Nation* on film. What are the benefits and shortcomings of each approach? How does each influence the audience's views on the subject matter? Using the discussion in the articles as a starting point, make an argument for using one approach over the other.

5. The final three viewpoints in this anthology discuss the Food Safety Modernization Act that became law in 2011. Critically examine the arguments in each of these viewpoints and decide with which author you agree. Do you believe that the act will improve food safety, as argued by Michael R. Taylor? Will the act have unintended, negative consequences, as Gary Wolensky, Anne Marie Ellis, and Kelly Regan contend? Which author makes the most compelling argument and why? Include quotations to support your stance.

For Further Reading

Marion Nestle, *Food Politics: How the Food Industry Influences Nutrition, and Health.* Berkeley: University of California Press, 2002.

Marion Nestle, *Safe Food: The Politics of Food Safety.* Berkeley: University of California Press, 2003.

Robert L. Paarlberg, *Food Politics: What Everyone Needs to Know.* New York: Oxford University Press, 2010.

Michael Pollan, *In Defense of Food: An Eater's Manifesto.* New York: Penguin Press, 2008.

Eric Schlosser, *Reefer Madness: Sex, Drugs, and Cheap Labor in the American Black Market.* Boston: Houghton Mifflin, 2003.

David K. Shipler, *The Working Poor: Invisible in America.* New York: Knopf, 2004.

Upton Sinclair, *The Jungle.* New York: Doubleday, 1906.

Peter Singer and Jim Mason, *The Ethics of What We Eat: Why Our Food Choices Matter.* Emmaus, PA: Rodale, 2006.

Karl Weber, ed., *Food, Inc.: A Participant Guide: How Industrial Food Is Making Us Sicker, Fatter, and Poorer—and What You Can Do about It.* New York: Public Affairs, 2009.

Bibliography

Books

Tanya Denckla
Cobb
Reclaiming Our Food: How the Grassroots Food Movement Is Changing the Way We Eat. North Adams, MA: Storey, 2011.

Paul Keith
Conkin
A Revolution Down on the Farm: The Transformation of American Agriculture Since 1929. Lexington: University Press of Kentucky, 2008.

Deborah Kay
Fitzgerald
Every Farm a Factory: The Industrial Ideal in American Agriculture. New Haven, CT: Yale University Press, 2003.

Bruce L. Gardner
American Agriculture in the Twentieth Century: How It Flourished and What It Cost. Cambridge, MA: Harvard University Press, 2002.

Lisa M. Hamilton
Deeply Rooted: Unconventional Farmers in the Age of Agribusiness. Berkeley, CA: Counterpoint, 2009.

John E. Ikerd
Crisis & Opportunity: Sustainability in American Agriculture. Lincoln: University of Nebraska Press, 2008.

Daniel Imhoff,
ed.
The CAFO Reader: The Tragedy of Industrial Animal Factories. Healdsburg, CA: Watershed Media, 2010.

Sandor Ellix Katz   *The Revolution Will Not Be Microwaved: Inside America's Underground Food Movements.* White River Junction, VT: Chelsea Green, 2006.

Nicolette Hahn Niman   *Righteous Porkchop: Finding a Life and Good Food Beyond Factory Farms.* New York: HarperCollins, 2009.

Carlo Petrini   *Slow Food Nation: Why Our Food Should Be Good, Clean, and Fair.* New York: Rizzoli Ex Libris, 2007.

Matthew Reed   *Rebels for the Soil: The Rise of the Global Organic Food and Farming Movement.* Washington, DC: Earthscan, 2010.

Pamela C. Ronald and Raoul W. Adamchak   *Tomorrow's Table: Organic Farming, Genetics, and the Future of Food.* New York: Oxford University Press, 2008.

Periodicals

Janet Adamy and Richard Gibson   "Flak over 'Fast Food Nation,'" *Wall Street Journal,* May 18, 2006.

Courtney Bailey   "Supersizing America: Fatness and Post-9/11 Cultural Anxieties," *Journal of Popular Culture,* June 2010.

Kelly Brownell   "In Your Face: How the Food Industry Drives Us to Eat," *Nutrition Action Health Letter,* May 2010.

Current Events   "Burger Battles," December 6, 2010.

Hannah Fairfield   "Factory Food," *New York Times*, April 4, 2010.

Andrea Freeman   "Fast Food: Oppression Through Poor Nutrition," *California Law Review*, December 2007.

John Intini   "Healthier, Whether You Like It or Not," *Maclean's*, December 25, 2006.

Kristin M. Jones   "Fast Food Nation," *Film Comment*, November–December 2006.

Anna Lappé   "Cafeteria Consciousness," *Nation*, September 21, 2009.

William I. Lengeman III   "The Other Fast Food Nation," *E: The Environmental Magazine*, May–June 2007.

Alice Miles   "In the Battle for American Stomachs, Big Food Still Wins," *New Statesman*, August 29, 2011.

Marion Nestle   "Reading the Food Social Movement," *World Literature Today*, January–February 2009.

Jennifer Ordoñez   "Fast-Food Lovers, Unite!" *Newsweek*, May 24, 2004.

Heather Paxson   "Slow Food in a Fat Society," *Gastronomica*, Winter 2005.

Michael Pollan   "The Food Movement Rising," *New York Review of Books*, June 10, 2010.

Marilyn Stranske   "Choose Your Poison: A Review of *Fast Food Nation*," *Social Policy*, Spring 2002.

Stephanie Strom and William Neuman   "McDonald's Trims Its Happy Meal," *New York Times*, July 27, 2011.

Bryan Walsh   "This Land Is Your Land," *Time*, October 24, 2011.

Index